ABOUT THI

Dean Fraser – The Quantum Poet is probably well known to many people these days for his radio show Beyond Poetry which he shares with over a quarter of a million listeners via a network of amazing community radio stations across the UK and beyond. He previously spent years touring extensively and continues to thrill at standing before an expectant audience ready to listen to his poetic tales...manna to his soul indeed.

He has also enjoyed his poetic musings being featured in New Dawn, Kindred Spirit, Culturium, New Age Journal and Fate & Fortune, to only mention but a few.

This collection brings together in one set of covers for the first time ALL of the vast number of poems from his seven poetic collections.

www.deanfrasercentral.com

Be they inspirational or thought provoking...absorb yourself within these pages and leave the cares of the world behind for a little while. The author runs workshops helping people to live a more auspicious life
PSYCHIC NEWS MAGAZINE

OTHER TITLES BY DEAN FRASER

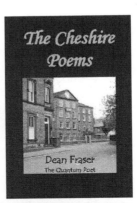

247 Poems

All the best

[signature]

Every Poem & Every Story for the first time brought together in one AMAZING COLLECTION!

Dean Fraser

The Quantum Poet

www.deanfrasercentral.com

Contents

Introduction

6 years' worth of my poetic output in one set of covers?

247 poems?

Wow!

I can only offer my deepest gratitude once again to you, my esteemed readers, that you enjoy my poetry and continue to venture along to see my live shows.

As 247 Poems was almost closing for publication, I wrote a new poem and felt compelled to include it…there wasn't room in the main body of the book…instead I have cheekily added it into part of my introduction…rules? What rules?!

Observed On My Travels

There it sits nailed to its tree
So long after the event…so long
A statement of intent to make
And yet the message was lost to me
Sadly, lost within their ignorance
Here we have a living thing
It has lived longer than you or I
Vital for our survival…essential
Wounded, yet still very much alive this tree
And how one rusty nail speaks volumes
As it holds it's now faded sign
VOTE FOR ME! Loudly it proclaims
Or something along those lines
They care about the environment apparently
So they say without a trace of irony
Vote for me?
No Thanks!

Enjoy the collection and say hello if I see you out there at a theatre or library soon.

Dean Fraser

Come Work in Our Factories

Long hours spent toiling the land, his family had done for
generations
Living in tune with the seasons, never thinking of other
occupations
Farmers his father and grandfather before him had been, what
else to be?
Of his sons he was proud, he said "one day you will take over
from me"

Come work in our factories, leave your village, leave your land
Come work in our factories, live in our town, live as we planned

1820 was the year, November the month it happened
He'd stored his grain for winter, his calf it was fattened
"Father we must leave, we're promised work in the mill"
Slowly the village emptied, leaving old timers and the ill

Come work in our factories, take our money, take your pay
Come work in our factories, work in danger, work as we say

Factories filled with young farmers along with their wives
Children knowing only noise and danger all their young lives
Living in the towns, surrounded by bricks and by stone
Their farms but a memory, now forlorn and alone

Come work in our factories, low income, low rewards

Come work in our factories, make us rich, make us Lords

Long hours spent toiling in factories, his family had done for generations
Living working men and women, never thinking of other occupations
Factory workers his father and grandfather before him had been, what else to be?
Until modernisation and mechanisation, he said "what will become of me?"

Come work in our factories, learn new skills, learn computers
Come work in our factories, live in villages, live as commuters

A story of firstly the industrial revolution and then the IT boom of the last twenty years.

Illuminated – A Brighter Kind of Vibe

A quest for spiritual enlightenment somewhat surprisingly found me in Blackpool

Admittedly a town better known for its decadence rather than existing as anyone's road to potential nirvana

Yet still my inner voice told me to go visit Blackpool, so I sallied forth one winter's day

And it was illuminating in its own way, at least once darkness descended

The world famous Blackpool's Illuminations
Explored this time on foot for mile after magical mile

A different kind of food for the soul…

Normally ancient landscapes attract me, this time I went for electric dreams

Boots 1

The boots are quite small to fit small feet
They are pulled on before sunrise
Sleep being forsaken, for there is work to do
And being late is out of the question
The boots walked along the well-worn track
To the place of noise and danger
For another day of clearing cotton fluff
Dodging the scary machinery that could crush her in a second
The dirt and smell sometimes making her retch
And yet she was grateful for the work
It kept her from the workhouse and that was enough
Enough to stop her from complaining
When her work was finished for the day
And she pulled off her boots for bed
She dared to dream…
Although she was only ten years old
She dreamed that if she ever had children of her own
That they would never have to follow in her footsteps
And work in the mill

Tells the story of my Great Grandmother who hailed from Coppull

Boots 2

He slept with his boots on
Although true sleep is alien to him now
A cacophony of sound disturbs his slumber
Fear being his daily reality
He had volunteered, the Chorley Pals they called them
His friends were right there with him, wanting to do their bit
He had been in the hell to which they sent him for only two weeks
And yet he had already outlived all his Pals
A veteran at 19 years old
Oh yes, he slept with his boots on
And he would die the same way

This is Great Grandfather's story; sadly it is not a long one...
This is dedicated to anyone who has lost someone through war.

Far from the Moderate Crowd

From time to time the need beckons
Escape, commune with nature
Recharge jaded batteries
Seeking inspiration I venture

The story is the same
It's always the same
Escape from wall to wall people
Solitude where are you?

Where in Lancashire?
For once to be truly alone
Ways to seek
Seek and you will find

November finds me on a beach
St Annes far out by the sea
Gales blow and I care not
Not a human soul to be seen

Oh yes, this is solitude
And so much more
Commune with nature?
At its wildest…just perfect

Driving rain pounds me
Waves loudly crash metres away
Wind threatening me
And I feel ALIVE

Inspiration inspired by inspirational nature

Amber

The street infused with an amber glow
Changing moods and colours into a twilight reality
Of half remembered days before
When night was dark and a panorama of stars stretched out across
the sky
All the constellations existing as everyday entities
The Pole Star…re-assuring in its certainty to guide the way
Whole Oceans being crossed using only the night sky as a map
Compasses being made into the landscape to plot the progression
of stars
Pyramids built with an eye to the position of Sirius, in the search
for immortality
To be out on a clear winters night
Far away from the amber light
Look up and see what our ancestors could see
To travel in time like the light from the stars

This was brought about by the view from my writing place window as I
sat seeking inspiration for a poem…

The Moon Looked Down

It was a clear night
The Moon looked down upon the city dwellers
Going about their important tasks with intense intent
Meaningful and yet oh so meaningless
Interconnectedness works overtime to make sense of it all
Fit everything into the quantum soup
Such strange ingredients to work with

Moon, what say you?
Looking down on those oblivious to your gaze
What do you think of us celestial guardian?
Is humanity the ultimate work in progress?

*A walk through Preston City Centre late night/early morning prompted
me to come up with this…one of several poems inspired by that walk…*

Sir Eric of Morecambe

I'm sure he would enjoy the view
If someone could think to review
Standing as he does there all the day
He needs to be looking the other way
If we could ask him I'm sure he'd agree
He liked bird watching, he should face the sea!

His statue on the seafront looks towards the town…

Flag Market Preston

So many changes
And still I remain
Magnificent Town Hall engulfed by fire
Yet still standing for many years
A half promise that it may be saved
But no…not this time
Crystal House, as was, seemed like a good replacement

So many changes
And still I remain
The Post Office building
Functional and yet beautiful
Still stands proudly yet obsolete
The cenotaph a reminder
Of the fragility of human life, but not humanity

So many changes
And still I remain
The Harris Museum and Library
Great centre for knowledge and reading
For the people of Preston
Creating a new horizon for the then Town
And now the City

So many changes
And still I remain

They build all around me
Changing the road layout
Buses no longer passing by me
I am the eyes of the City
I am the Flag Market

An open area at the heart of this Lancashire City which has never been built upon, plans exist back to the 16th Century showing this to be an open space. Here the Flag Market gets to tell its own story

1970's Preston Outdoor Market

1970's Preston Outdoor Market
In memory was always busy
Vibrancy
Full of characters
The banter passing back and forth
Between customers and stall holders

My mums mum worked there in the 1970's
Selling clothes come rain or shine
And often frost
Standing on cardboard to stave off frostbite
Fingerless gloves
And a headscarf

Mint imperials
She would carry a large bag of mint imperials
Why was the mystery
Especially as she never ate sweets herself
I asked
A winkingly knowing look my only answer

1970's Preston Outdoor Market
Now but a memory
As is my mum's mum

Yet still the mint imperial mystery
Well, I asked my mother
And it's finally solved…

Her bag of confectionary
It was never for eating
It was all about pigeons
Sitting in the roof above the market
Mint imperials thrown to scare them away
Stalls remaining pigeon "message" free…

And a mystery finally solved

Railway Bridge

Radio Lancashire now main reason for visiting
Quoting prose or rhymes I've been scribbling
Back in the day took my partner to visit the town
She got quite bored, looking at me with a frown
Rivets are the reason, they caught my attention
Victorian railway-bridge, well worth a mention
Standing in the rain, viewing the construction
Falling in raptures…genius my deduction
My partner not quite sharing my glee
Getting quite wet, looking daggers at me
"Can we go get a coffee? She dragged me away
From the beautiful bridge that had led me astray

A tale of Blackburn

The River Ribble

Full moon reflected in its mirror like surface
The sun creating crystal sparkles
Dancing magically all around
Ancient watercourse way
Tamed a little, but still wild and free
Once, long ago, large ships would navigate their way to the docks
Fast becoming a recollection lost in the mists of time
A story now told through fading photographs
Fading group memory
A place of rocks and whirlpools
Danger within the serene waterscape
Sometimes flooding homes
Reminding humans they are quite small compared to nature

*Starts in the hills of Lancashire, making its way to the sea at Lytham St
Annes. From time to time it likes to remind people it is there…*

What is Good About Bolton?

She said
"What is good about Bolton?"
An honest enough question…awakening memories
Memories of my journey to the glamorously named Gas Street
The former Reebok Stadium standing as an artificial landmark
Time to leave the superficiality of the motorway…

The Romans must have built the road into Bolton…mile upon
mile of perfectly straight bumper to bumper travel at 30mph
Nearing the town, passing impressive educational establishments
Traffic signals on red…waiting and looking around
Part of the industrial landscape of fine Lancashire
They were once mills…now serving as warehouses, shops and
even homes…

This market town…it always seems busy
Taking the turning towards my destination
Visiting Barry Roberts and his dog Becky…both good friends
Commerce and business taking place over conversation and
banter
Wondering if they ever built the promised Superstore on a
levelled Gas Street?
Brushing the past under yet another layer of concrete

Came about when a friend and I were discussing the merits of various different towns. At one point she said "but what is good about Bolton!?" which made me think that there is a story to be told here!

Limerick in Lancashire

There was a woman from Preston called Dee
Who was sensible to the highest degree
She stayed away from clubs
Never to be seen in pubs
And she never once thought she was a bee

Why is This Town Not Full of Painters?

Always a mystery why artists don't see
Open spaces, wonderful light at the sea
Seascapes, observation of life, the view
Brushes and canvass inspiration renew

Climbing the only hill in Fleetwood
The Mount, exercise can only be good
Beautiful buildings, architecture, the sky
Why I'm not tripping over painters, I always wonder why?

A Town Re-Born

What happens when commercial fishing starts to die?
Fleetwood never looked back or wondered why
A choice, a community is renewed and reborn
Retail therapy the way forward the town to adorn

Shopping now awaits at the end of a tram journey.

And **A TOWN RE-BORN** *both talk of the small coastal town of Fleetwood*

My Life in Pilling (Aged 9)

PART 1

Pilling beach is beautifully flat
And usually peaceful and tranquil…but not today
A roar of machinery being tested to its very limits splits the silence
There is nobody else around…just the sound of an engine
And the boy riding along the beach…throttle wide open
Low down over the handle bars…as he tries to extract every last horse power
From his…moped!

PART 2

City life in Manchester had been exchanged for the rural village of Pilling
Suddenly he realised that hens and cows are where his eggs and milk came from
That tomatoes grew in hot houses and money could be made by offering to help harvest them…this alien environment had its advantages!
A village school for this alien intruder from the city to attend
Talking with children who lived on farms indeed eye opening
And yet, all they wanted to know about was the city

The story of what it was like to move from the big City of Manchester to a very rural seaside village in Lancashire

Knott-End-On-Sea

Trying to stand upright
Yet the gale force winds have other ideas
Icy cold rain finding its way through many layers of clothing
Eyes half closed in protection
Look across the water to Fleetwood
Not many people around today
Although a container ship unloads its cargo
Wondering what the crossing must have been like from Ireland
Perhaps they are used to it?

Walking
No, running along the seafront!
Aided by the wind in his back
To buy chips
Seems like the thing to do at the seaside
Holding hot food, warming frozen fingers
Sitting in the shelter…eating
Storm raging all around…thinking
This is a day I feel truly happy to be alive!

Resides on the Lancashire Coast

Different Pace of Life

Lancaster Canal she lived upon
Or was she berthed there?
Can never really decide
Why are boats always "her"?
Eighteen years she *resided* there
Providing home to her guardians
Shelter, home and hearth
All life going on
Around and within her
Journeying Preston to Garstang
Taken at walking pace
Somehow so civilized
Watching motorway traffic
Frantically rushing to destinations afar
Enjoying drinking tea at four miles an hour…

Lancaster Canal was once home to an Aunt and Uncle

Supermarket

Super marketing
Promotions offering
Now less than half price
Luxury range is twice as nice
Free wine with every ready meal
Buy one get one free, what a deal
10p off washing powder
Save on our bean chowder
Giant store dominates the landscape
Spend now, there can be no escape!

This tale was actually written in a very busy supermarket; not really my natural habitat.

Once Upon A Time

Once they were great
Maybe even the best
Cups and medals
Once they proudly had Tom Finney

Once they played to a packed stadium
Every single home game
Everyone in Preston a supporter
Once they were amongst the elite

Once they had the Museum of Football
Just for a little while
Taken away
Once they were feared

Once they had a dream
Make it back to the top
Once...just this once...they might just do it
And they can again be great

*Is my tribute to the late, great Prestonian, Sir Tom Finney - a true
gentleman on and off the football pitch.*

His Home Town (For Brian)

It started with a craving for real black puddings
And true Lancashire cheese
To walk the streets of his youth once again
Look up old friends
Visit too seldom seen family

Like most places do given forty years
Preston had evolved, changed
It took some time for him to get his bearings
The house he was born in
Now residing under a car park

The tram bridge on Avenham Park
A point of familiarity
The water rushing by on its way to the sea
Just as he had all those years ago
Jumped aboard a Jamaica bound boat

The beginning of a life of true adventure
Taking him around the World
Too many stories to tell
Some other time perhaps…
Wandering this half familiar town

Winckley Square, sitting on a bench
Less trees, he observes
Once this used to be his playground
Smiling at the memories
Beginning to feel more alive

Finally venturing into the indoor market
Buying kilos of black puddings
And crumbly Lancashire cheese
Taking them South with him
Back to the town he now calls home

Is for my much loved Uncle. He set out from Preston as a teenager for a life of unimaginable adventure…

Where Did It All Begin?

You'll find it in the Doomsday Book
If you care to take a look
Different spelling of the name
Still plain to see, all the same
Going back through the mists of time
Where it all started, hard to define
Countless generations in the past
Humans with vision create something to last
A ford, a hill and a settlement came
Penwortham they thought made a good name

Written originally for an event in the town

Roses

When I first heard of the War of the Roses as a small child
I imagined it must be all about two gardeners who hated one
another
One obsessively growing red roses and the other equally
passionate about their white ones
I asked at school ….."it isn't about gardeners; it's about two
houses, Lancaster and York"
This one confused me even more…I now viewed ALL houses with
great suspicion!
Looking out of the window at the other houses in the street….it all
seemed very sinister
Of course, I grew up, learned about history…this cross Pennine
rivalry thing going on…and on
The conclusion I have come to…Lancashire and Yorkshire in the
21st century…it's really all about cricket

Everyone Wants A Parking Place

In Chorley, first time in many years
Could it be all as it now appears?
I know everyone wants a parking place
Yet there is puzzlement upon my face

Seems from where I stood and observed
Chorley apparently is more than served
Car parking covering more square feet
Than every shop in Chorley, on every street

Upon parking and disembarking
On the warm spring day, walking
The Flat Iron Market I espied
I said I wouldn't mention it, I lied

Upon reading a little of Chorley for an event I had there, I noticed many before had written of famous local people and especially about the strangely named Flat Iron Market. I determined to do something different…

What Do I Know?

His more spiritually inclined lyrics have been known to attract my
attention.
Jon Anderson voice of legendary progressive rock band Yes hails
from Accrington.
Does his home town hold some hitherto untold mystery?
It was to be my mission to uncover the whole picture.

I have explored the streets,
Felt the energy…erm…man
Experienced the actual real vibe of Accrington
Concluding…
Well, the past it's alive here
Victorian mill buildings
Railway arches definitely beautiful.

Oh but what of the mystical experience I hear you ask!
…weeeeell…okay there wasn't one…
Jon Anderson must have been born with some kind of spiritual
awareness or else it came from exploring outside of the town.

Next time it's going to be the natural landscape around Accrington...next time, there is always a next time.

I sometimes enjoy seeking inspiration in the less likely places...no disrespect intended to dear Accrington but I don't recall reading many stories about truth seekers necessarily making a beeline for the town. Or perhaps they do and I am the one in the dark here? Anyway, back to the story and the reason for my seeking out this fine example of a Lancashire town, which is strangely more to do with music than anything else.

Sat Nav?

Is there a sat nav to find your car?
Lost again, it can't have gone far
Happens every time I visit Blackburn
Really would think I would start to learn
Take notice of the zone in which I am parking
Would save such trouble in disembarking

The parking zones at Blackburn never seem to fail to confuse me, I really
ought to make a note of which zone I have parked in

Garstang Through The Years

Earliest memory
Feeding ducks that seemed out of a children's story
Waddling around and eating the offerings made to them
Outgrowing the pushchair
Walking along the cobblestones
Singing Simon and Garfunkel songs with my mum
Changing words and feeling "gravy" rather than groovy
A time of innocence and exploring

Years later living in Singleton
Travelling to Garstang
Market day
Traders vie for attention
Fruit and veg, clothes and electrical goods
Seems anything can be bought
Enjoying the hustle and bustle
A time of commerce and growing

2014 sees me retracing steps
Another time, same place
I write this poem specially to perform
Imparting to others my experiences in their town
And yet I am compelled to add this verse
After the event
Garstang and I, soul mates perhaps?
One day I shall return…one day…

Pre-school I lived in Garstang and periodically have re-visited the town, last time was as a performer for a Festival in the town

Talisman For Leyland

Man in bronze frozen in time
Silently he observes Leyland
Once the market was a factory
Here he laboured
Lorries and buses
Cast by his own hand
Just as he was
To remind the people

The sculpture on Hough Lane

Lancaster Times

City centre intact still largely survives
Beautiful buildings a feast for the eyes
River Lune eerily shrouded in mist
Move here or not, the thought does persist

From Williamson Park looking down
Past the Castle to Morecambe town
The sun rays glistening on the sea
Like a million jewels shining magically

Looking to move to this fair city
Yet all the cars seem such a pity
I wonder if it will ever come to pass
They'll finally build a Lancaster bypass?

A few years ago I toyed with the idea of moving to Lancaster, I like architecture and the City has some fine examples

Aviation Salutation

It nearly became part of history
A footnote in Blackpool's story
Quaint yet essential in its functionality
If you've ever been through, you'd agree
Friendliest example of its type out there
Existing by hard work, a wing and a prayer
As a new era dawns I'm happy to report
The continuing survival of Blackpool Airport

It was close to being all over...

Kiss Me Quick – Tangerine Dream

Standing next to the library a gallery of art
Nourishing the soul, culture they impart
Paintings, sound, all arts it embraces
Taking us to many far away places

Streets a mix of Victorian architectural hints
Mixing harmoniously with all the glitz and chintz
What should be a total clash somehow blends in its uniqueness
Becoming quite sublime to the senses in its completeness

The greatest giant of this Victorian dream
To copy dear Eiffel was part of the scheme
Far seeing sentinel overseas the town
Catch the show, see the creepy clown

Stayed there myself when I was quite small
Stood there and tried to take in it all
Said to my parents, whatever it takes
Can we leave this place and go to the lakes?

Another, this time, slightly irreverent look at Blackpool, I do love the town really, well sometimes!

No Animals Were Harmed in the Writing of this Collection

Vegan is about more than a lifestyle choice
It's eating and living by my own inner voice
Although I wouldn't wish to cuddle a cow
It's nice to know I don't eat them anyhow
Pork chops I feel should remain on a pig
If I need extra protein I'll just eat a fig
There is a downside to living cruelty free
Visit the health shops, view the prices, you'll see
I wear shoes without leather, belts made from plastic
Vegan is all or nothing and some think too drastic
For me it works and I never ever preach
A decision 25 years ago I decided to reach
So if you've had a burger we can still have a conversation
Just don't describe your lunch expecting me to react in elation!

I always like to include a vegan poem in each collection, never to preach or attempt to convert anyone...more by way of an affirmation

The Diligent Parking Man

Of course, it helped that he looked exactly like Oliver Hardy
His lack of a Stanley, doing nothing to undermine the hilarity
Parking his car the mission, you'd think it would be easy
Yet I'm laughing so much I'm starting to feel quite queasy
No parallel parking here, the last spot on the end of a row
Yet how many trials Oliver felt compelled to undergo
Crawling at a snail's pace, backwards his Nissan travelled
Tie flapping in the breeze, out Oliver climbed looking baffled
Distance checked, back aboard he inched backwards again
Then forwards, as if not quite sure exactly where to aim
Door opened, waddling, he sagely took yet another view
Smiling to himself, parking one more time to now pursue
Reverse engaged, even more cautiously Oliver proceeded
Yet thirty slow seconds later, he felt another view was needed
Out he got again in all his glory, prudently weighing distance
Through tears of laughter, I had to admire his persistence
A metre of room at least, within which he might manoeuvre
Motion returned and he really couldn't have done it smoother
He'd parked! Without the rear of his car being remodelled
A final smile of satisfaction, locking doors, off Oliver toddled
How about the owner of the car he diligently avoided bruising
I rather doubted they would find his actions quite so amusing
After twenty minutes Oliver got his Nissan oh so neatly parked
With 5 millimetres between his and the car he'd left unmarked

The action related here happened one sunny afternoon as I looked from my creative space window out onto the street below

Adult Education...Probably

How the heck did this come about?
Apparently there is no way out
A man's got to do what he has
Plus other clichés and all that jazz

Okay be brave, how bad can it be?
Well I guess I'm going to shortly see
Keep thinking positive, it'll be over soon
Imagination ran wild all afternoon

Parking outside, few short steps inside
Perhaps they won't notice if I hide?
Okay here goes, one small step for me!
Last chance gone to escape, be free

Walking around the place of education
Talking of exams, targets, expectation
After all I came here in a sense to learn
Parent's Evening soon over for another term...

Returning somewhere I imagined I had left behind

The Longest Poem

Seek YOUR Truth and set yourself FREE!

I usually end my shows with this one...

Exercising Mind, Body and Soul

Beeston Castle is a ruin now
Once proudly standing atop its hill
Now a pay to view tourist attraction
Still appealing nonetheless
Our past facsimiled into stone
The lives of ancestors
Tuning in, as ascent is made
Walking and feeling
Hours spent communing

And then a picnic
Overlooking rolling Cheshire countryside
Carrots are munched
Hummus enjoyed
And then peaceful inspiration
Seems the flat rock is made for our purpose
Sun on our backs
Journeying inside
The perfect place for yoga

Where It All Began

Revisiting childhood memories
Going back…right back to where it all started
I'm a writer now
They enjoyed my stories then
My first venture into the education system
Northenden, South Manchester
Now I'm back again after all these years
Or is it a moment?
Difficult to be sure…can we ever be sure?
The performance and an audience anticipates
They arriving fashionably early to talk with the troubadour
Asking of his inspirations and motivations
They always like to know these things…
After the show I go
Walking the streets my former self once trod
That's not right is it…former self?
I'm still me
Same brain…more or less at least
I think therefore I write
Looking at the education establishment
Otherwise known as my first school
Fine Victorian architecture I can now appreciate
How do I feel?
Sad for a long lost childhood?
Hardly…it's alive in me
It's being a writer you see

Imagination needs to be nurtured
Like a child or an adult
Use it or lose it
That old cliché holding true
Northenden my home for five years
Has it changed? I'm not sure
Memory plays tricks on us when it feels like it
I like this place. Did I always?
Not in the sense I would wish to reside there you understand?
It helped make me who I am

Great Truths Revealed

Upon first living in fair Macclesfield
Gradually great truths became revealed
"Macc" everyone talked of all the time
Why do I not know him, give me a sign?
"Who is Macc?" I asked a local I know
"Macc is the town!" I just answered "oh"

Where have all the people disappeared?
Empty shops, some even closed, weird
Footsteps echoing through empty mall
Phone a friend…and she told me all
"Where's everyone?" I asked uncertainly
Her answer left me no wiser "Barnaby!"

Learning of local slang and public holidays

Prestbury - The Honourable Thing to Do

Hay fever season announced its usual presence
 Sneezes with sore blurry-visioned eyes
A charity cricket match and I'm invited
To play, of course
Prestbury Cricket Ground is beautiful
And full of grass
Freshly mown grass
And for sure it is hot
Pollen count off the scale on the day
Streaming eyes rendering me out of the game
My sneezes might distract the batsmen
Just not cricket!

A compromise reached
Run the scoreboard
Actually understanding cricket helps
I do, of course
Sitting in the midday sun
Dosed full of homeopathic remedies
Beers appear for me periodically from the pavilion
Gently, slowly falling fast asleep...
Suddenly the shout goes up
Game over...everyone looks across at me
"Why are there no scores on the board?!"

Two teams of players heatedly crowd round me
"Oh…erm…as it's for charity I thought an honourable draw
would be the fairest result!"
And they seemed happy…

They Used to Throw Witches From Here

The whole area awakening into spring
Buds forming on trees along with fresh leaves
Daffodils shoots climb their way from slumber
Soon this place will be a kaleidoscope of colour
The scent of nature coming alive fills the air
In anticipation of new life
And I heard they used to throw witches from here

Finest woodland resplendent in summer
The sun indiscriminate in sharing its warmth
Families exploring and enjoying this place of leisure
Access for all to share in the beauty of the scenery
Views across the whole of Cheshire and beyond
Stood near the Edge of Alderley Edge
And yet they used to throw witches from here

Sensory overload with the approach of autumn
Magical the scenery thrills in red, gold and green
A grandparent searches for his misplaced grandson
He is quickly found with happy tears and smiles
The scent of the trees while kicking up leaves
A lingering impression on the senses
And still they used to throw witches from here

Snow covers frosty trees in the heart of winter
Thinking back through time and it seems so close
When wise women of the village or the eccentric
Misunderstood or considered some kind of threat?
If they lived they were guilty, if they didn't innocence
Either way to be accused meant the end
And they used to throw witches from here

A year in the life of Alderley Edge, Cheshire

A Break in the Wall

A busker plays piano accordion at the cross
Incongruous or perhaps that's me?
Here to retrace the steps
Of my ancestors?
Well...no not really
Unless they were Roman?

Where was I?
Retracing steps...yes
I have been here before
Oh years before
Resided a stones throw away
Walking the wall

There are ghosts along this wall
Of my own making
Memories
Conversations
"Memories are made of this"
Dean Martin once sang

Italian interlude again
Needing to exorcise the ghosts
Book shop still there
Nothing for me
Nothing

Moving on

Sentry tower stands
Former look-out post
I hear voices
Whispered
Remembered
Give me silence

Horribly modern interlude
Steel bridge
Straddling dual carriageway
Wall demolished
Making way for cars
Progress apparently

Chester Race Course
No horses today
The Dee passes by
Traffic intrudes
Again
Leave me alone

Back on the wall
Cathedral in site
More ghosts
Straying inside
Voices again
Back to the wall

How many times?
Circuits around Chester
Remembering
Looking forward
At the past
It's alive here

All too alive
Ghosts of Deva on a wall
Gold once found here
Or love?
What goes around
Comes around

Dedicated to all the women I have suggested going for a walk around Chester walls with…at last I poetically salute you!

Mud Is Mud and Trees Are Trees

They say it's sanitised, somehow less than real
All too carefully managed, not the real deal
Non-native trees they feel a bit synthetic
A visitor centre in the forest, well just pathetic

Smiling people all ages, always happily say hello
On foot, bike or horse into the forest you should go
Blakemere Moss was landscaped, wildfowl unaware
Like anyone who's seen the lake, I doubt they'd even care

Oh the scent of fir trees on an autumn afternoon, bliss
Yes, it has changed, evolved if we dare to reminisce
Does it actually matter, a forest resistant to disease
Mud is still muddy and trees after all are still trees

I used to live nearby Delamere Forest in Cheshire, the arguments are
probably still going on about the way it is managed

Honesty Box

Looking from the window patiently waiting
Though it seems like forever it's taking
Vast fields of ripening sweetcorn inching higher
The farmer has said "take all that you require,
You'll find the honesty box there by the gate
Leave what you think you should, all will be great"
Finally it arrives, the day it's all ripened, ready to eat
Getting the pan ready and sprinting across the street
Picking four beautiful, succulent corns to savour
Straight in the pan, preserving every gram of flavour
Simply eating, simple food, simply incredible
Making supermarket corn seem almost inedible
The farmer found ten pounds in his honesty box
A small price to pay for a meal that totally rocks

Is what rural life in Cheshire, England was like just twenty years ago; I wonder if it's still the same today? I like to think so...

Ghost Hiking?

High above Macclesfield Forest
One late Saturday afternoon
Against a wall I leant to rest
Thinking it will be dark soon

The Cat and Fiddle pub just in sight
As stretching weary limbs I pondered
Enjoy a beer as day turns into night
Convivial time not to be squandered

Brought back to reality, daydream over
"Gutten Morgen!" a passing couple said
Smiling back greetings to my fellow rovers
As slowly it began to register in my head

Being wished good morning at 7pm
A little odd whichever way I looked at it
To retrace my steps, find out more about them
Taking their path and then it finally hit

Open moorland, not a soul to be found
They passed me just two minutes before
Yet no Germans or indeed anyone else around
Only one possible way to go, I set off to explore

Walking thirty minutes, emptiness answers back
In the twilight I have the moors to myself for sure
Where did they go, any other way there is a lack
Only one explanation, however obscure

In August on the moors above Macclesfield Forest
As I pondered visiting a favourite pub of bikers
Leant against my wall enjoying as I did my rest
I met a couple of German ghost hikers…

A true story of walking all day and then a surprise awaiting me…

Chester Railway Station 2007

Activity abounds all around
Hustle and bustle
People lending extra action
Extra stress
Cars attempt parking

Travellers soon to be train-ward bound
Madness of arrival
And even more departure
The cacophony of taxi horns
A car strayed onto their "patch"

Hurried hugs of loved ones
Friends air kiss
Not a moment to be lost
The queue to park grows bigger
Car drivers jostling

Finally find your seat
Booked in advance
Soon beginning to unwind
The Cheshire countryside flashes by
Leaving on a fast train

The Lesser Spotted Soccer Player

For ninety minutes a week centre stage is theirs
Every move scrutinized, fans offering up prayers
"Get the ball in the net!" "Stop them from scoring!"
As one the crowd united in chants they're roaring

If soccer players be your main source of excitement
You can view them in their natural environment
No need to peep through gates or over their hedge
Just go hang out in a wine bar in Alderley Edge

Oh, I used to see them all when going for a meal in fair Alderley Edge,
regardless of if I wanted to or not! I even recognised some of
them…without my companions discreetly pointing them out

Flashes at The Bottom

"You really must visit The Flashes" they eagerly said
Some strange thoughts now running through my head
"ooookay" I replied "where exactly do I have to go?"
"The bottom of town, you can't miss 'em, you know?"

Off I went through Winsford to see what I would see
An open mind often helps I've found particularly
You don't know the town, The Flashes secret I will share
A nature spot, a beautiful lake and nothing at all that's bare!

On The Mic (Not!)

Two ambitions now fulfilled
Wishing to do something poetic there
Determined to enjoy every moment
Located in Chester Town Hall Square

Promoting the cause of libraries
An event I couldn't possibly miss
Town Hall steps my platform
Should have been an hour of bliss

Sharing my words with Chester
Creating my usual poetic ambience
Cheshire based words flowed forth
But where exactly is my audience?

The sun shone down, the square beautiful
One gentleman at least looked me in the eye
As he asked for directions to the library
As I watched dozens of other people rush by

It seems my new friend had the best idea
"Shall I follow him?" I pondered
In search of an audience to hear me
To the library I also wandered

Located by the entrance poeting
Lovely people gathering listening
Words once again flowing forth
My audience finding them riveting

My afternoon in Chester was terrific
An experience I will never forget
I'll be back again some day soon
That I didn't bring a PA system my only regret...

Chester and a lesson learned. Never fun being unheard...

Remembering

Some truths are hard to conceive
Beyond what I'm able to believe
The joy remembered as tears we cried
How is it 35 years since Ian Curtis died?

A man who once lived in Macclesfield, this poem was written in May 2015

And I Never Knew Her Name

She bit into the green apple with perfect white teeth
Is her hair really that shade of red? I suspend disbelief
Smartly dressed she stands, all the world her stage
Happily serving anyone coffee she earns her wage
She sees all life going on, smilingly serving drinks all day
She must have heard it all, chatted up in every possible way
Managing to look like the coffees she sells really matter
As the mall cleaning woman stops by for a friendly natter
Caught off guard, just this once, stepping away from duty
Eating her apple, leant against a pillar, flame haired beauty

A guardian angel in Ellesmere Port who kept me plied with hot drinks,
while I performed poetry for two hours outside her coffee shop as part of a
library promotion event

Never Gave Much Thought to Knutsford

The best way of knowing
Taking in the sites
The history
Modern life co-existing perfectly alongside the past
These old buildings still live
Occupied and appreciated
I smile
I'm here to take photographs
The occasional tourist?
No, not this time
A new town guide needed
My job to capture moments
Freeze frames of life going on
Published and shared for posterity
Marble Arch with pretty flowers
Mrs Gaskell's house
Church and Ruskin Rooms
Tatton, Italianate Houses
And everywhere else on my list
All suitably recorded

Never gave much thought to Knutsford
Formerly only part of my journey to the M6 North
Until today

Now we are inexorably linked…

Marble Arch, Knutsford

Never gave much thought to Knutsford…and a photographic assignment changed all that

Macclesfield Canal

It doesn't sound too promising at first does it?
Yet it's wonderful; let me expand a little bit
To walk the canal is to travel in time
A golden age of industry, pure sublime

Macclesfield canal… never seen anything so amazing
For hours standing transfixed, admiringly gazing
Can a work of civil engineering so add to the panorama?
Functional, yet with unearthly beauty…pure drama

Starting out from Macclesfield early one morning
Strolling through our industrial past, rain pouring
The journey taking me by beautiful old mills
Against the backdrop of the Peak District hills

As I read the Guide that I'd bought
I saw how the people had fought
To keep alive this great canal of heritage
Victorian Engineering centre for pilgrimage

People still live on the canal, the legacy carries on
Marina of brightly painted boats I come upon
Pondering, I almost consider life on the water
A thought left behind as to my flat I saunter

The past made large and brought alive once again
When I'm at the canal does it always have to rain?!

A Pinch Of Salt?

Digging down they found their goal
Prehistoric man like a human mole
Pits dotted across the Cheshire plain
Their prize worth all the toil and pain

Industrial revolution then came the mines
More evidence of those fast changing times
Men still toiled, but now beneath the land
As extraction plans continued to expand

Vast caverns of cathedral proportions
Easing icy roads of maximum importance
Deep down under Cheshire so mineral rich
And why so many town names end in "wich"

Cheshire has been mined since prehistoric times, although the legacy is not without its problems

Wich or Wych means brine pit or salt rich

Alternative Tatton Hall

The day is beautiful
Sun resplendent in clear blue sky
Happy smiling faces look out of car windows
As we walk past deer
Birds welcoming us with song
Observing from their trees
On a day such as this
Stillness, warm and just a little magical
Driving into Tatton seems a shame
Strolling brings new experiences
Unnoticed by the many
Scents and sounds, sensory delight
Eventually commercial encounters
Joining the throngs of the craft fair
Acquiring hand painted cards
Watercolour originals worth braving crowds
Then culture can wait no more
Into the Hall we venture
Our picnic cannot come with us
Left in safe keeping
As through history we browse
Peeking into lives and ways of living
We answer the invite of the gardens
Nature embracing us once again
A tree is climbed, well a little
Don't tell anyone...shhh

Backpacks retrieved walking resumes
Searching for the spot
An oasis of calm in the height of summer heat
The canopy of trees protect us
Meditation and then food
A rabbit watches us
"Hello fellow lettuce munchers!"
He seems to say
And then in an instance he is gone
We linger a little longer
Talking and reading
Watching cars leaving in the distance
Against the heat haze they queue for exit
Later when they are all departed
In the early evening sun
Steps are gently retraced
Taking our leave of Tatton
For now…

I guess we all get what speaks to us out of any experience

Once They're Gone

Irresistible the two hundred year old mills
I would love to collect them in all honesty
Like Clough William-Ellis made Portmeirion
I would have my own industrial history village
Silk, cotton and any other mill is welcome
I would rescue neglected gems of architecture
The derelict, unloved, soon to be demolished
I would restore them to their former glory
This was our ancestor's world, let all see and learn
I would be preserving a forgotten way of life
Let today have its retail parks, built upon history
I would adore being able to follow my dream
A vision of the past for future generations
I would also appreciate the funding, thank you kindly!

That is what is I find so wonderful about some older areas of Macclesfield and indeed certain other Cheshire towns; the industrial buildings have moved with the times and are still being used today.

Views of 1980's Macclesfield

Dario Said

I would see him in passing sometimes
That rarest of men in these modern times
On my way into Crewe, he'd be working
With his team on their way to training
Embodying loyalty, commitment, action
His job some wouldn't see the attraction
Unsung hero, admired throughout the game
Modest self-deprecating man all the same
Let me shout out my appreciation for all to see
And hear it for the one and only Dario Gradi!

"The legend" a part of Crewe Alexander football club for over thirty years

Lymm

The sun always shines down on Lymm
Do they never get the weather most grim?
Kind of place it's impossible to feel down
Happy smiles all round, it's that kind of town

It always seems to be sunny in Lymm...

Gone Nuclear

Cold War raged
Future uncertain
Those mad times
Place of refuge
For the chosen few

Fast forward
Metamorphosis
Transformed
Once deadly serious
Glimpse what might have been

*The not so secret nuclear bunker in the heart of Cheshire, now a visitor
centre*

Crewe Shining Bright

Let's hear it for 1837
Pure railway heaven
Crewe junction
Beautiful function
Where it all began
Engineer's big plan
The hub, the heart
Victorian state of the art
Locomotive construction
Century of production
Living, breathing history
Every brick tells its story
Billions have passed on through
The railway station at Crewe

Crewe railway station is one of the most historic in the World and although functional is also a thing of beauty (to me at least!)

Warrington

Excitement ran the through the class
"We will go on a school trip next week!"
"Great" went up the shout "a day out!"
If only we knew the truth, so to speak

As town hall gates go, kinda cool they certainly seem
Definitely deeply gold; enough bling for any rap star
An hour the gates were studied by us, every detail
Why did they chose to bring us here, rather bizarre

Coach journey of forty five minutes undertaken
Facts reeled off, rejected when new by Queen Victoria
Eventually gifted to Warrington and now we can view
Teacher in raptures, not really sharing her euphoria

Warrington is a pleasant enough place
Least that was the opinion of me and my mates
The mystery being why it was a good idea
Bringing us to study deeply the Golden Gates!?

A school trip once undertaken by yours truly to view the iconic gates of the Town Hall; perhaps not quite able to be truly appreciated by my teenage self

Dreams to Follow

I like bridges and piers, in a parallel World I'm a civil engineer
in this World I am mostly civil and mostly sincere
I like architecture, in a parallel World I designed Arley Hall
In this World I just sketch buildings, taking in it all
I like trains, in a parallel World I drive them through Crewe
In this World no leaves or snow on the track will do
I like trees, in a parallel World I planted Delamere Forest
In this World against a tree I simply like to sit and rest
I like canals, in a parallel World whole regions I slowly cross
In this World even how to use a lock I'm at a loss
I like folk music, in a parallel World I'm in Fairport Convention
In this World poetry is my way of getting attention

*My thinking here is that we all have dreams, yet how many of us have
the courage to pursue them? I am particularly pleased to get Fairport
Convention as guests in one of my poems...this is a theme I returned to
more than once*

Solitude Where Are You?

The story is the same
It's always the same
Escape from wall to wall people
Festivities, trivialities
Desiring a different experience
Hear my heart beat
Truly breathe
Solitude where are you?

For once to be truly alone
Ways to seek
Seek and you will find
New Year's Day finds me in a forest
Far from the moderate crowd
Rain lashes down and I care not
The allure of wildness
Solitude where are you?

Driving downpour pounds me
Branches offer scant protection
Wind cuts through me
And I feel ALIVE
Not a human soul to be seen
Be at one with nature

Gaia at her most extreme
Oh yes, here is solitude!

Macclesfield Forest on the bleakest of days – magnificent!

Retracing Steps

It started with a desire to walk those streets
The one's the less worldly me once walked
I left a part of myself there it seems
Time to reconnect, reclaim
Look up old friends

Like most places do given fifteen years
Macclesfield had transformed, changed
Taking a little time to get my bearings
The market has moved it seems
Old location now resides under a building

Chestergate, a point of familiarity
Once cars travelled here, no more
Freedom to walk unhindered
Grosvenor mall, salad baps from famous bakery
Just like all those years before

A bench, sitting pondering and eating
The faces in the town may be unfamiliar
Some things never change
Beautiful buildings feast for any eyes
Hills still protectively overlook

Walking the 108 steps in both directions
Feel the past under my feet

Mine and thousands of others
Cobbled streets with their own story to tell
Some other time perhaps…

Yet this is never nostalgia
Oh no, anything but nostalgia
The town has evolved, moved on
Just as I have and once did
Cheshire is in my heart…always will be

A trip I made a few years ago to all my old haunts in Macclesfield

Admiration Of Tarporley!

You see I'm really rather fond of Tarporley!
Not for the reasons most people would see
Oh it's pretty, cute shops, clearly well heeled
My admiration altogether much more left-field
Why I like Tarporley, with my exclamation mark
It's home to the raceway at great Oulton Park

When I tried the Oulton Park Circuit I was the fastest poet round the track on the day…well okay I was the only poet!

Alderley Vigil

Do we hear a voice gently whispered?
Could it be we're guided by the wizard?
Cave explored, as bravery will allow
Turn back! Get out of here right now!
Spooked emerging as sun sets down low
Rightly accompanied by squawking crow
Magically atmospheric darkness descends
Everyday world fades, mystery transcends
Flickering shadows cast as torches flaming
Branches swaying skeletal fingers playing
Strange noises pierce surrounding darkness
Eyes strain seeing all enveloping blackness
We light a fire, but keep that to yourselves *
Oh the mystical night of wizards and elves
Stay we will 'till the sun rises once more
Embraced within landscape ancient folklore
Midnight exploration time our reckoning
Clouds part, moonlight bathing beckoning
"Explore by my light, keep to the paths mind!"
Spring walked by, are we alone, someone behind?
Eerily, warily, awareness stretching outwardly
Onward continued ever more determinedly
Impossible conveying our experiences logically
Affecting us in different ways psychologically
They say King Arthur waits deep inside the hill
For his time to come again, by power of his will

Eight hours later, daylight slowly replaces night
We take our leave, agreeing Arthur just might…

A night spent outside at Alderley Edge a rather long time ago…

* Please don't go lighting fires in the countryside!

Now Truly Living

With pure open heart
Negativity can now depart
In beauty to be walking
Inner voice talking
Cleansed, feeling whole
Mind, body and soul
Harmless ways of living
Caring and easily giving
Projecting what's inside
All eyes open wide
It's easy to really fathom
It's about Love in every atom
In every action, every thought
The still point that is sought

Freedom To Forgive

Experience, past actions trapping us into actions
Locked into ways of behaving in our reactions
Dealt with according to the rules that we make
Surely a pattern we would rather now break?

Unlearning habits created throughout our life
Ways of being, causing ourselves and others strife
Letting go of no longer needed baggage the way
To practice forgiveness every moment of every day

Firstly, forgive ourselves for mistakes we made
Mistakes are only discovering how to not behave
Then starting to forgive other for every mistake
The hardest part of the journey we chose to undertake

Actively practicing forgiveness, the greatest favour we can do
Bursting out of comfort zones, our life to continuously renew
It won't happen overnight, give it time, wait you'll see
Happiness from deep inside, then at last you are free!

The Spark Of Understanding

Why is it thought such a fight
Living life within the light?
Purely expressed feelings actual
Emotional balance is only natural
There never was anyone else to blame
Personal responsibility to now reclaim
Life being ours to make of what we will
Thinking purely, truths, freedom until
Our future to be shaping and moulding
Parallel with our learning unfolding
The spark of understanding
Within us all, now expanding
Why is it something so many appal?
The simple fact that love is all

Chitter Chatter

Chitter chatter please cease
Give the world some peace
Inane pointless natter
Gossip radio patter
Careless words spoken
Constant stream unbroken
Robotic clichéd meetings
Unthinking smiling greetings
"How are you, are you well?"
Feels like I've died and gone to hell!
Can we not really talk anymore?
Truly communicate…I implore!
Look past the superficial
Surely will be beneficial
To really talk to one another
Never know what we might discover
A proper conversation?
Yippee! Pure elation!!

Aiming To Live

Think deeply about your ideal utopia
your perfect vision of your own life
as you always dreamed it can be.

And be honest with yourself here
nobody said everyone's dream needs to be the same
find yours and that is what you aim to live!

Less Than Perfect

The people we love sometimes will not be exactly who we wish
them to be
they make what seem to be mistakes, yet are all part of their
growing and their own personal journey
decisions they make
experiences they go through
sometimes makes us question
if we really know them
if they are worthy of our love.

It may change who they are in our eyes
yet can our judgement have been so wrong?

If we perceive them to be a certain way
this is OUR reality of who they are
in OUR experience of knowing them.
how seem to be to us.

If we want to keep the reality
which is real to us
never an illusion
of who the person was or is to us
we need to accept them
faults and all
accept that people have many facets
yet our own relationship with them was

or is good
and forgive them for being less than perfect sometimes...

Gossip Every Day

Gossip, thoughtless mindless prattle
Words for words sake do hum and rattle
Who did what, with whom and why
Makes me bang my head and cry
Causing their personal chain reactions
Slings and arrows by their own actions
Listening to all this with an inner sadness
Why can't they get the cause of their madness?
What we put out into the Universe
Straight back at us in reverse
Negativity creating more negativity
Time to take personal responsibility
Positivity creating more positivity
Always the choice for humanity
Listen to our words and what they say
They create our reality every single day

Each And Every

It is part of every doctrine
Every religion
Every philosophy
Every metaphysical knowledge
Quantum physics
Occultism…
Ok, you get the idea
All the wise ones say the same
We ARE what we think
Literally
Words resonate through time and space forever.

The Cliff Face We Face

To climb without ropes, no safety net
Without fear, hardly breaking a sweat
Sometimes to reach the peak, take in it all
Sometimes be careless then the fall
Landing with a thud and then pain
Walking in the sun and the rain
It could be said without the spills
We wouldn't be equipped to enjoy the thrills

A Living Cliché

To try to achieve, will be just that, trying
Trying is never achieving, better we believing
Attempt to reach our goal, attempting being
pro-action
A World of difference between the two, attempting gets a reaction

Putting our-self down, scared of life, shake and cower
Training a new way thinking that's all about energy and power
Failing is a myth every time only shows another pratfall to avoid
Next time lesson learned a new pathway now deployed

Success they say many things to many women and men
Surely success is being happy without hurting anyone and then
Listening to the inner voice we can finally understand
What makes us happy have our future's in our hands

Life is about the path we take towards inner empathy
Harmony and the still point sure you would have to agree
Follow your bliss so they say many a truth spoken in cliché
Take the first steps right now you know inaction is so passé

The Sand On The Beach

We can read all the books in the world on spirituality
On personal development, ways of achieving immortality
Listen to as many gurus and self-help masters of lifestyle choice
As there are grains of sand on the beach! There is a quiet voice
The true path is still to look deep within, all answers already
known
Meditate and look within, gently find our own way home

All The Things

It being absolutely essential
To live our life to our potential
Drifting along, getting on by
Lazy ways to truth deny
Living this way being soul treason
Finding excuses, rhyme or reason
Looking away from where we should be
Closing our minds to our liberty
My reality took a while to sink in
Inner voice screaming, making a din
Quantum spirituality my path to take
Safe, boring life I had to forsake
Thoughts...words...emotion
The message of love, deep devotion
My role in life was to spread
Heart for once ruling my head
As I go about, my mission, my task
An audience to listen is all that I ask

The Hustle

Hustle can be a positive word
turn over every stone
send those emails
network with the more experienced
knock on all those doors
set aside plenty of seriously fun thinking-outside-the-box-time
seeking those far-out methods to generate ways of getting yourself
where you deserve to be as quickly as possible.
Ask and then ask some more…"

Art Of Being

To fathom all the depths
The art of being
Harmonious communication with every atom spiralling
The multi-dimensional way of truth
The river so to carry
Intuition intelligence
Emotional maturity
Existing beyond dimensions
Simultaneously exuding love
Living within love
Limitless…

Now Is The Time

The most wonderful way to experience all the magic
The magnificence that is called life
Is to live in the now.
For the moment...it is the only reality

Buy Out To Buy In

If you spend more than five hours a day
watching television
imagine what you might alternatively do
with those thirty-five hours in a week
to actively create a different, more fulfilling, life for yourself…

An Awakening

Let your thoughts soar
Your words encourage and enlighten
All your actions be pure and wise
Living in peace and harmony
Growing through learning to be free
Feeling only harmonious emotions
Your silences a clarion call of purity
Anything is possible…anything

Noise Vs Quiet

Trying hard to lose my mind
Rationality limiting intuitions potential
Still the thousand random thoughts are vying for attention
Yet meaning nothing
Try meditation? Possibly...
And yet the thoughts are still there later
Do be quiet mind and let me think

Trust You And I

Trust intuition and it will guide you in the right direction for you.

There are some experiences we do need to go through however bizarre they may seem at the time, later it does tend to become clear exactly what it was all about.

Understanding our relationship to our planet and seeing the landscape as a living evolving entity, which we are all inter-connected with.

Learning to respect nature and her mysteries is all part of starting to feel through our intuition

Gaia

Love and interconnectedness...
Energy powering through every cell...every atom
Let's make it the energy of universal love and harmony
Balanced and centred
Gaia needs us...

Everybody Say Yes!

Opportunities are presented to be taken
it is up to us to grab them by both hands, tweak life on the nose a
bit
and see where saying "yes" can take us!

George Inspirational

Brainwashed by white noise
Brainwashed marketing ploys
Brainwashed by the masses
Brainwashed in the classes
Brainwashed out of thinking
Brainwashed into sinking
Brainwashed blocks the soul
Brainwashed no longer whole
Brainwashed by the day
Brainwashed work for pay
Brainwashed pay the bill
Brainwashed makes us ill
Brainwashed see them walking
Brainwashed eating talking
Brainwashed by the hour
Brainwashed take your power
Brainwashed in our beds
Brainwashed vacant heads
Brainwashed into buying
Brainwashed soul denying
Brainwashed words are spoken
Brainwashed fractured, broken
Brainwashed is all around
Brainwashed put you in the ground
Brainwashed who put us there?
Brainwashed do we care?

Brainwashed no longer
Brainwashed we are stronger
Brainwashed turn away
Brainwashed make your day
Brainwashed become free
Brainwashed live, love, just be

Where To Look

The big wheel is apparently not a wheel, but an eye
Boxes of people suspended in air and time, up in the sky
The panorama stretches out before them, the city laid bare
A few million souls living, they look like ants down there
Which way to serve them best?
North…South…East or perhaps West?

There is culture in this vast metropolis, but is anything real?
Find a place to go, chill and soak up the real deal
Concrete, glass and steel glinting in the midday heat
On Terra Firma once again, time to go vote with their feet
The overwhelming need, no choice, they cannot wait
They know where there is culture, they will visit The Tate

There is art in this City…

Most Alarming

Alarm Clock.
To me that signifies an emergency or a calamitous event which
might be about to happen to get quite alarmed about.
Most Alarming.

Wake Up Call.
Each day my clock is still ringing, yet now my Wake-Up Call sets
me off into a day full of motivation and possibilities.
Rather than alarming my nerves.

Zoning Out Zone...

Who is controlling them?

What do they listen to?

Why do they have to tune out of life?

Out of nature and all around them?

Ignorance seems to be their bliss

Is it all the same tune or is it subliminal messages they receive?

I see them all around every time I walk out of my door

In the city, the park, the library, forest, up a mountain

And I wonder why

Why

Why

Why do so many people now seem to walk around wearing headphones?

Ever Expanding

Interconnectedness of all things
humans, flora and fauna
Gaia
atoms
everything we say lasting forever
recorded in the akashic records
and in our bodies
illness caused by nothing
and nobody
but ourselves projecting negativity
everything we put out there into the Universe...comes back to us

Metaphors

When all is done and said
at the end of the day
the game of two halves
taking the rough with the smooth
with our shoulder to the wheel
whilst scraping the bottom of the barrel
and dealing from the middle of the deck
getting off my cloud
in any sky with diamonds
getting a round hole with a square peg
eating an apple that has a worm hole
teaching the old dog new tricks
where the horse has been led to the water
and when Beethoven perhaps rolls over...
we can choose to evolve through love
or not...

And Now The Sports News...

A soccer team won out against another team and they are quite happy about it.

Cricket...two teams played one another, it took days and only a small handful of people really understood the game and what's happening.

Rugby news...a bunch of muddy guys beat-up and jumped all over another bunch of muddy guys, while throwing around a mis-shaped ball and then they went home.

Let's Talk

How we communicate with others
those vibes we send out.
Our personal power
creates our life
our relationships
our World
energy, pure and simple.
Chi
Prana
lifeforce energy.
Our emotions sending out these waves of power all the
time...creating and manifesting...us

Pruning

An ongoing process towards light
To simply be, is my delight
Pruning and cutting out of my life
Negativity, darkness, causes of strife
Moving forward with a lightness of touch
Feeling deepest bliss, Universe thank you so much

Evolvement

Evolvement comes from living.

Making mistakes which are not really mistakes but learning.

Walking our talk and sometimes tripping up along the way a few times.

Before we finally get the message about what we need in order to grow.

Shedding old patterns of behaviour as we progress through life, rather like the snake sheds its own skin to renew itself.

In The Zone

So, what exactly is a comfort zone?
It's those fears and illusions we face alone
Pushing through what we think is possible
Self-imposed limitations highly probable

To no longer have a comfort zone
Growth being a journey we face alone
Discovered through experience anything is possible
Just do it, success is highly probable

Calm

Whenever times became challenging
Life not going according to wanting
She only had to look within for comfort
Then was the time to become inert
Her ancestors running through his DNA
Guiding her path every moment of every day
Inner wisdom of ages to call upon
Negativity depart and begone

Words of Magic

Trying to fathom the meaning of words
Words of meaning
Words of power
Words with thought
Words that cure
Words that curse
Words heard in passing
Words creating karma
Words of strangers
Words are names
Words carry magic
Words as swords
Words once spoken
Words remain forever
Words that resonate
Words create our lives
Words make us who we are
Words time to take heed
Words careful what we say
Words spoken in haste
Words remembered by the Universe
Words are our life manifested…

Endless Possibilities

Confidence comes from inner knowing and can often be mistaken for ego...
ego dissolves through lessons in humility...
humility is recognizing that everyone is born equal...
equality is sending love to all regardless of their actions...
action is to consciously change first ourselves and then the World...
Worldly is to completely know oneself...
one...
To be at one with oneself

We are all here to grow...only expectation brings success.

Emotions

expressions of emotional energy
   through thoughts
 words
        music
  art
    poetry
     when created with love
          are immortal

Forgiveness

the past trapping us into emotional patterns
similar situations when encountered
dealt with according to the rules WE make
for better or more often worse
for us

unlearning habits of negative reactions
different people bringing new opportunities
letting go of no longer needed baggage
carried for far too long and now irrelevant
forgive firstly oneself for mistakes made
Then forgive other for their mistakes

open up the doors of our heart
And be absolutely free

Collected Works Of The Poet

Freedom from ego and false pride is freedom from the chains of our karmic see-saw
Living within the energy of conscious creation seeing the signs as they are shown, which they surely will be.

Passing the point of intuition, to reach the point of initiating what will be and being open to the consequences of those decisions.
Accepting, with grace, all that crosses our path.
Seeing it as it TRULY IS
Another grateful opportunity for growth.

Beauty Of Life

Return to innocence...be as a small child...look around and learn from nature...see the sky...feel the breeze...the sun on your back...the stars at night...infinity within and without...such beauty...such beauty

The Same Thing Anyway

Our perception of reality
Our place in the world
Reality bubbles
Peering outward
From fathoms deep within

Sometimes overnight
Maybe a lifetime
Or more than one
Dismantle our own bubble
Take a good long look at you

Then the world
Created around and within us
Transformation underway
Re-learning
Awakening from spiritual amnesia

Unfolding
Serious dedication
Much work
Once the bubble is gone
Change is inevitable

See it through
Exist as a free being

Life and reality
Our own or the universe
The same thing anyway

If I Take My Leave

If I take my leave of the green green wood
Home to Herne the Hunter and Robin Hood
Sunlight finding its way through the branches…magical
A living breathing ecosystem starting with the botanical
The symphony of nature provided by operatic birdsong
Natural balance perfecting, every creature does belong

If I take my leave of the green green wood
Would it cease to exist? I wonder if it could?

If I take my leave of the mountain top
Rising into the sky like it will never stop
The sunset transcending anything seen before
Reflected in the mirrored lake on the valley floor
Strongest winds attempting to dislodge me to a fall
High upon the mountain, sitting taking in it all

If I take my leave of the mountain top
Would it cease to exist? I wonder could it stop?

If I take my leave of the blue seashore
Small waves sometimes tranquil, other times a roar
The sun creating magically sparkling light all around
Unmistakable fragrance and the unmistakable sound
In a bay far from people, for once truly alone
The seabirds diving in and out of the white foam

If I take my leave of the blue seashore
Would it cease to exist? Can we be truly sure?

Did I create these natural places in my own minds eye?
Every tree, plant, animal, the sea, sun and even the sky?
If humans are unable to appreciate freely given beauty
Simply stand and gaze in awe at all of nature's bounty
If we cannot look around, cherish all Earth has to give
Would WE cease to exist? Would we really wish to live?

The Man From Huddersfield

Halifax or Volkswagens in my mind eternally associated
The Classic Beetle Centre above the town located
Passing mills, terraced streets, to slowly climb the hill
Ancient engine eventually arriving like Jack's friend Jill
Overlooking the town, industry and people symbiotic
Whichever way I looked at it, couldn't be called exotic

Huddersfield later with a friend, we catch up sometimes
Professional globe-trotter sourcing minerals in mines
We talk of my visit to Halifax, describing a certain mill
 "Aye, Halifax, it looks just like when I visit Brazil"
So there you have it, if to North Yorkshire you go
The experience is identical to visiting *Rio* de Janeiro

The story starts in Halifax though…

Waterproof

Standing stones, an avenue of them welcoming
Silent guardians and I'm walking, questioning
"Why do I not feel the energy, man?" hmmm mysterious
Palms outstretched hug a stone, nope seems I'm oblivious
Neolithic sites magnetically draw me like a moth to flame
Avebury third time here "still no vibes, man" what's the game?
Some of the stones are missing of this I'm completely aware
A few now concrete posts, signifying what was once there
Don't get me wrong, I like this place, ancient pub in the middle
Yet why I fail to feel a thing, I've yet to solve the riddle

Avebury, Wiltshire inspired a few poems, this is the first

Jacques Brel Would Be Shocked

Anticipation
Waiting to be shocked
Well perhaps a bit
Glimpsing the wild side of life...for a little while
Train station looks remarkably ordinary
Still...the city awaits there!
Follow the people to excitement
They turn right from the exit
In their wake we go
Hey, this can't be right?
M & S, BHS and H & M
We could be anywhere!
Amsterdam is wild, everyone says so!!!
"Canal Taxi!" we hailed
This is more like it "Show us the sites"
With a knowing look to the driver
And he does
Endless canals, bridges and more boats
People riding bikes
Past a gaudy bright green ship
And we're through with the tour
Dropping us and going
Is this the "real" Amsterdam now?
Looks promising this narrow back street

Door of a seedy looking club opens
Stone cold sober Brits stroll out
Chatting politely about Uni
Where is the action here?
Observing was to be our mission
Staying on the edge
All life going on
Signs lead towards the centre
Reluctantly so do we
Oh sure they have hemp cakes
Remarkably civilised it all is as well
Where is the wildness?
Sailors Jacques Brel sang of...
Different age I guess
Everyone plugged into music
Or sending texts
Too busy with technology
Debauchery consigned to the history books

Amsterdam

Beautiful Rusting Place

Port of Liverpool fascinates watching from the beach
Industry thriving amidst the hive of activity
Sound travels on the breeze

Wind farm dominates the seascape, blades turning
Working in harmony with nature for once
Power to the people

100 silent sentinels cast in iron looking out to sea
Made in the image of their creator so they say
Taking the water twice a day

A sunny day at Crosby Beach and the Antony Gormley sculptures

Central Park After Dark

Late night arrival JFK Airport, what to do next?
Got my baggage, been through all the security checks
Wait here until it comes light the sensible decision
Sensible? A thought I greet with abject derision
A journey at night on the subway in New York City
To miss on the opportunity would seem such a pity
The guidebooks say with greatest caution now proceed
If proceed at all, bad people prey on the unwary indeed
I'd dressed down for the occasion, anticipating such a trip
Oldest coat, tatty hat and back pack, the full "street look hip"
Boarding the subway car attempting to avoid attention
Sharing it with the weirdest dudes I'd care to mention
The roughest looking one asked me if I had the time
Showing him my bare wrist, "No" I tried to mime
Thinking I'll keep to myself I tell time by my I-phone
Satisfied I wasn't worth mugging he left me alone
Arriving at my stop, time to leave my new friends
Checking in after ten hours travel, body now to cleanse
One shower, a change of clothes and it's still only 3am
Deciding to explore, find somewhere to eat and see then
All night grocery store anything there for me to eat?
Something vegan, avoiding dairy, eggs and meat
Buying orange juice, a bunch of grapes most green
I'll find somewhere great to eat or my name isn't Dean
Where else is it the Guidebooks scream we must avoid?
Central Park after dark, my plan is now deployed

I'm only two blocks away, to Central Park I did wander
Why I like to live so dangerously others often wonder
Sitting on a bench munching grapes quite contently
Drinking juice made from concentrate equally happily
Feeling strangely safe there even at half past three
Not that I ever felt in danger, rather completely free
After my first adventure in the big apple eating fruit
To bed and some slumber I thought would be astute

Manhattan Pt 1

The Guggenheim

Walked through Central Park along 5th Avenue
Destination we'd read so much about coming into view
Standing back gaping at the alien architecture before us
Incredible building, sallying forth anticipation all abuzz
Worth the entrance fee to simply look upward inside
Enough procrastination, let's go see art, we decide

Never given much thought to Van Gogh not strictly my scene
Face to face with Vincent in a frame, passion in extreme
Maximum respect to the man who felt compelled to cut off an ear
Genius a description never used lightly, we can see it clearly here
Viewing his paintings need to push on through a crowd
Vividly he depicted his world, painting loud and proud!

Cezanne…erm, sorry people I fail to feel inspired or even moved
If I could be so insolent to suggest it could so easily be improved
I'm a surrealist and I totally get that whole impressionist thing
Cezanne's blobs of colour entirely fail in making my soul sing
I've seen where he painted, the magical views and light
Maybe I miss the point, my loss I guess, she said "quite"

Gazing upon works by Manet, Monet, Renoir and Picasso
Complete sensory overload and we've still three floors to go
A room devoted to Lucio Fontana asking the question why?
Ripped canvasses stitched with string, weird off-the-wall guy
Was he saving on paint or totally mad, who cares or knows?

Jackson Pollock was kinda cool though, his style, anything goes

One floor to go now, some things becoming obvious
Three weeks spent here would never get monotonous
Inspiration on every wall, in every frame, every room
And some day we'll come back again, can't be too soon
The overwhelming memory apart from the art that's neat
There's something about the floor completely kills your feet!

Manhattan Pt 2

Everyone Gone Hostelling, Hostelling USA

People brought together from every walk of life, every nation
Sharing space, pots and pans, stories…romance and flirtation
Amsterdam Avenue HI Hostel our temporary home
A base from which around Manhattan we roam
Setting out each morning, another museum or gallery of art
Cooking and enjoying the three lounges, a story I'll impart
One giant TV playing Friends constantly all the night and day
Resplendent bean bags to recline in, while the hours away
The basement lounge pervading odour of an old training shoe
Strip lighting, vending machine, pool table, not for us thank you
No TV or background stench third lounge our natural choice
Not much at all in there, just some comfy sofas, we rejoice
Passing time in conversation, chatting with whoever and who
Meeting some of our fellow visitors, like us just passing through
An Aussie, seems I'm his "mate" he actually called me "blue"
French guy who'll chat up anyone with a pulse, mon dieu
All life goes on here, a Brit who arrived in 2000 and stayed
Hippy couple from Germany, into free love and fair trade
Larger than life Californian, blonde, bearded surfer dude
Getting dressed, Japanese girl, middle of the dorm, nude
Seeing is believing, not that I took that much notice obviously
Deeply absorbed as I was in my conversation…erm, honestly

Manhattan Pt 3

Rhododendrons And The Hudson River

Unexpected botanical specimens appreciated as we wait
Rhododendrons growing wild, well untamed at any rate
We want to see it after dark, adding textures, night views
Navigated Hell's Kitchen, towards our Liberty Cruise
Flowers near the ferry office, she takes photos up close
Standing back I admire, a poem in my head I compose

The tour starts, Liberty awaiting our pleasure
Our Guide talks of real estate prices, work and leisure
New Yorkers who wouldn't live anywhere else whatever
The Big Apple gets in your blood, a tie you can never sever
And he's right. As we cross dark water, a starry sky above
Oh yes, here is a City of which you just have to fall in love

And there she stands, on her Island, her torch held high
Billion of photos exist already, cameras click as we pass by
More memories made, more images of Liberty, of course
"I never get tired of her" guide declares. A view I endorse
Camera cards holding images like so many times before
Tour over all too soon, another experience, back to shore

Manhattan pt4

To Travel More Pleasurable Than Arriving?

Politely I claimed to suffering from mal de mer
Seasickness in extremis, don't even go there!
My phobia of large ships having been safely overcome
Storm force gales hitting our ferry and I'm all undone
Portsmouth to Guernsey seemed like such an easy jaunt
It's just the pitching and rolling making me look so gaunt

I had looked forward to standing on deck, taking in the view
Plans that went quite spectacularly entirely, madly askew
Instead I saw four walls. Small cubicle in which I resided
Unable to leave no matter what motivation I provided
Here I would sit until our three hour crossing is complete
Impossible to leave the gents, though it would be kind of neat

The ferry arrived late. Next stage of our journey now awaits
Guernsey, our Sark connection heading out harbour gates
Seems we'd need to find different means to continue on our way
Can it really get any better for us on this terribly thrilling day?
Two hours later, wild storm, who'd be mad enough to go to sea?
Oh we found out who, thus continued the nightmare journey

A lunatic I shall call Phil, offered to take us to his home Isle Sark
Without thinking too deeply we agreed, we'd arrive before dark
Happily Phil announced "this could get a little rough, hold on!"

Waves fathoms higher than the boat, any moment we'd be gone
In the cabin Phil manfully clings to his wheel, grinning madly
Our life in his hands, wanting to reach that safe harbour badly

The biggest wave of all threw me in the air leaving my seat
Then with the deck my posterior did non too tenderly meet
Phil scooped me up with one arm, still steering his fine tub
Telling me how he'd buy me a drink later down in the pub
Finally we arrived, Sark safely moored, on dry land and how
Crumpled on the floor bags, tent and me…I'm still alive…wow!

Starting to go dark now, our campsite we must find with haste
Quickly up the hill, by tractor, with not a moment to waste
Paying the owner of the site as the sun is finally setting
And we need to pitch our tent, oh joy, I was nearly forgetting
Finding what seemed to be a nice quiet place up went our tent
Closely followed by me in my bag and fast asleep I went

Morning brought all kinds of new experiences
Place we'd pitched defied all logic and appearances
There was a very good reason for our tent being alone
Dark hiding many things, our predicament unknown
When we saw our location thinking "what if?!"
Pitched half a metre from the very edge of a cliff!

The Channel Island of Sark

A Captive Audience

How about an Island with not a single car?
Where anywhere you want to go, is not too far?
Bikes and feet the way to get around the place
A relaxing life, taken at a much slower pace

Sounds about perfect to me, wonder if you agree?
So perfect in fact, I just had take myself off to see
Beautiful scenery, beautiful people, you really ought go
Would I want to live there permanently, not really, no

The answer to that question is clear to see
Apparently I'm a professional performer of poetry
An audience consisting of few hundred people, all told
I've a feeling my stories might start sounding a little old

Sark again…

Pass On Through

The bleakness of concrete and glass
Executed without thought for the aesthetic
Only functionality yet no functional beauty here
Gateway to everywhere it seems
Cheap consumables abound
Perfectly supplying a throwaway world
Yet perhaps there is substance?
Some deeper soul with history?
Constantly overlooked by bargain hunters
Or those only beginning their journey into mainland Europe
Long overdue investigation
To look behind the vulgar facade
A town existed before all this
Is it still alive?
On foot exploring…seeking answers
Oh there is a town after all
The centre from where all this began
Hidden behind warehouses
All streets have been walked and known
The answers sought crystal clear
A town bleak as all the concrete and glass
Nice railway station…these things are noted
And that's all

A visit to cultural Calais or perhaps not…

Un Baton *S'il Vous Plaît*

12th century Belfry, oh the history
City wall atmospheric in the sun
Overlooks protectively the old quarter
Suddenly out of nowhere
A cycle race on the road below!
Hundreds of bikes jostle for position
Fifteen minutes of noise
Then they're gone, silence descends

I'm going to be shown a surprise
The unexpected
Even more unexpected than the cycle race?
Adore the old quarter like Chester or Canterbury
We walk down the High St
Hunger pangs
Only one choice really
"Un baton s'il vous plait"

"Don't eat yet" she advises
Strolling further
Stopping
Staring
Where are we again?
Are my eyes playing tricks?
A seafront straight out of brochures
But how?

Whose idea was this?
Surreal
Like discovering Narnia in a suitcase
70's style hotels resplendent
The "beautiful people" topping up their tan
Reclining on golden sands
Finding a quite spot we sit
Munching on bread

Boulogne, French Coastal surprise

Town Of Books And Bowls

Quite appealing in a quaint kind of way
All generations, together, bowls they play
The square dominates, anyone for a game?
Scotland's Book Town so they proclaim
And indeed books shops are far and wide
Yet I'm entranced by the singular view outside
Everyone in the town plays bowls so it seems
Toddlers, farmers, the retired and even teens
In Wigtown they relax in the sun, play and talk
Occasionally stretching their legs the pub to walk
Conclusions are reached observing the happy smiles
Everyone should play bowls all across the British Isles

Wigtown, Scotland

Diving Off The Pier

Forgoing the train, tourists have it too easy
We'll walk he said, not that far, you'll see
Longest pier in England did he say?
Feels like it on this hot summer's day
Still I'm not complaining, I'm one of the privileged few
Getting to view what the tourists could never dream to do
My Uncle Brian works here, it's with him I now walk
Passing our stroll in silence, neither of us do small talk
Finally the end in sight, past attractions we continue
Down steps to a different world usually hidden from view
Diving kit lines the walls, Brian talking with his mate Len
For one day only I'm joining the pier maintenance men
Well at least that's what I thought, apparently not today
Diving boots, helmet I try on…then we leave to my dismay
Seems to dive from this pier you need some qualification
A license, welding experience, a course on resuscitation
I'd seriously thought in diving gear he'd let me in the sea
Wind-ups Brian's speciality…yet one more time he'd got me

Southend on Sea and all is not what it seems

Arbor Low

The circle marked with white limestone
Fifty slabs like cards that have been thrown
By some giant dealing out his giant deck
The Derbyshire landscape to bedeck

To sit within the circle, reaching to the past
Those Neolithic builders, a legacy to last
Arbor Low as the sun rises in the sky
The reason it was built, still to wonder why?

Warm sun drying the stones and the wet ground
Why they built the place I think we've finally found
Was it for sacred burials, mystic rituals, defences from attack?
No, it's because the ditch around it makes a great running track!

The story of an early morning visit to this ancient stone circle, deep in Derbyshire. And yes, that really is exactly how the experience all unfolded that day. Who knows, perhaps our theory was right?

Distracted Upon Avon

It came and landed right on my knee
Most beautiful dragonfly you ever did see
Keeping very still we looked one another in the eye
Then it seemed with a wink, it flew away into the sky

Nearly a hundred years ago you'd have seen a gondolier
Writer, Marie Corelli, on the Avon, quite the pioneer
Causing such a stir as she floated elegantly along
This Venetian taxi always attracting a smiling throng

Locks on the river need to be seen to be believed
Amazing what the Victorian engineers achieved
Chilled, happy people relaxing in the sun
And I'm nearly ready to leave, almost done

Remembering why it was I chose to travel here
To see the birthplace of William Shakespeare
Yet natural beauty and wonder here I've found
Never mind, Will, I'll catch you next time around

Tells of a visit to the town of the birthplace of a rather famous playwright and poet…

Beautiful Garden

Anne Hathaway's cottage stands awaiting our pleasure
Yet the gardens are divine in the midday sun
An arbour invites lingering
Playing word games
Rose of Eros
Orange of No Rage
We could live here
In this garden...

Another visit to Stratford upon Avon and still distracted...

Blinkered Response

Three times I had been Edinburgh bound
Three times I had driven along Princess Street
Three times several hours spent in the City

Then came the fourth time to venture forth there
Then came the question "what did you think of the castle?"
Then came my answer "what castle?"

Fifth time I kept my eyes open and looked around me
Fifth time I finally observed it
Fifth time there I wondered how I could have possibly missed it
the previous four times?

Edinburgh, Scotland

171

Getting Comfy

The weather was closing in
Horribly closing in
Landing at all as much in the air as our Airbus
Looking out the window at ice caked wings
That's as far as I could see
Visibility as good as zero
Our pilot speaks reassuring words of comfort
"We're gonna attempt to land, we'll be fine folks, enjoy the ride"
Descent begins
Hardly daring to breath
Someone nearby is praying
Perhaps that made the difference?
Touching down and taxiing
Sighs of relief and whoops of joy
We were the last plane to land that day
Our pilot being brave or reckless, he got us down either way
Formalities dealt with, next to home
"Due to the extreme weather, all trains are cancelled"
Looking three times at the notice to be sure I fully comprehend
What now?
The queue to hire cars stretched out from the Avis office
Not for me today thanks
No camping out in a rented car all night waiting to move
Trapped by the weather just the same
Thousands stranded here
Information desks all helpfully closed

This is Heathrow after all
My fellow adventurers' sitting waiting
Lateral thinking time
Sleep desperately needed
Tannoy announcements every 3 minutes
Hmm…escape to quiet?
Peaceful
Undisturbed
"No further flights tonight"
Came across loud and clear
"Roger to that!" a decision made
American Airline's Executive Lounge
Ahhh, comfy chairs an unlocked sound-proof door
Couldn't have asked for more
No staff around asking me to leave
And no tannoy, yes!
Bliss
Settling down in the lap of luxury
Full nights sleep later
On a coach heading to Watford
Onward by train
Would I ever visit Heathrow again?
Managed to stay away so far…

A night at Heathrow Airport

Leaving An Impression To Last

There is cold and then there is Ingleton on wintery days
Icicles hang magically from roofs, glisten in the sun's rays
Permafrost probably a metre deep, ice storm starts raging
Yet somehow I'm finding all of this alarmingly engaging
Quite determined to look around the village come what may
"Wrap up warm, sure I'll be just fine" optimistically I say
Looking in my car for extra layers to add and wear
Minus 15 degrees, my body will then be able to bear
Finding some sports kit pull it on over my current clothes
"Just a little stroll and see," the suggestion I now propose
"Go yourself" she said "I'll keep the car warm for you"
When I have to explore I've got to go, what can I do?
Walking through Ingleton in icy rain, people are staring at me
Coming out of shops making sure they believe what they see
Photos are being taken as rain falls heavier, my actions tracked
Mad cricketers rarely pass through there in December...fact
My cricket gear only extra protection I could add to my attire
If I said I made the local newspapers I wouldn't be a liar
Impression I left is I was possibly acting for some kind of movie,
Maybe a ghost, time traveller or simply an old fashioned loony

The story of a visit to Ingleton Village in the North of England

The Ancient Tree

A thousand years or more it's lived so they say, at least
Centuries before it became guardian for the deceased
These ancient builders of the church all knew
The magical and deadly power of the yew

Locked deep inside the secret of immortality
Pure poison within the yew, result fatality
Sitting in quiet contemplation, "tell me fine tree
A thousand years lived, what did you see?"

Do I hear a whisper on the wind, a rustling of leaves?
"I've seen good people, the poor, beggars and thieves
I've heard battles, preachers, the happy sing a song
I've seen it all, for to this landscape I belong".

Looking at the church again, some five hundred years old
And then at my new friend the yew and if I might be so bold
Good yew made sure the church, by the power in its leaves
Was positioned just so, offering shelter from that northerly breeze

Whatever humans plan, thinking themselves clever
The yew tree knows and will perhaps go on forever

A visit to Oxfordshire with a friend, who happens to be an expert on
trees brought about this tale. It imagines that a yew tree that has lived a

thousand years must have amassed some wisdom, on whatever level trees operate.

Gordano Services M5

I adore Gordano Services
Stop even when I don't need to
Love the community
The accents
Village life
Always the same

They have a milk float there
The old electric kind
Eco friendly before it's time
What does it do?
Empties the trash cans
Irony or maybe not

Village like motorway services
Freeway if in the USA
Yet this is Bristol
Well nearly
Yes, rustic it surely is
A one-off

Creation of a community
Temporary home from home
Road weary travellers
Have a coffee
Quickly eat some fast food

Play a fruit machine

Speed humps in extremis
Better take it easy there
A family plays catch-ball
It's that kind of place
You know?
Happy times

Fashionably Different

Half reluctantly I agreed
Well, how long could it last?
A tour of the Fashion Museum
Could even fascinate…maybe

Compromise makes life happier
She smiles, so do I
Entering an unknown World
With an open mind

Entranced…in her element
Enthusing, sharing knowledge
Exploring along with her
I see her point

Cultural history sewn together
Real people wore these clothes
Bygone ages coming alive
I share her passion

Fascinating time in Bath

Isle Of Cars

Crossing the bridge
Views across the island
New cars awaiting inspection
Then departure
Bound for the roads

Parking in the village
Viewing the main road
Newest car I seem to observe
Apart from mine
Was made before 1970

Sheppey in Kent

Once More To The Desert

Noise. A relative cacophony of noise fills aching ears
They're having a good time apparently
24 hour party people…yay!
Yet will they remember or even care later?

Needing to escape I take a walk in the desert
Water, sun-block and a good book…desert bound once more
I would spend a lot of time walking in the desert over those seven
long days…it became my…well…deserted home from home

The nightmare of package holidaying on Tenerife

Where To Look?

Pondering the question...
How to be inspired?
Meditating, dreaming
Mind works overtime looking for the answer
Information meltdown time

Taking a quiet moment...looking around seeing anew
Inspiration?
It's in every tree...city life goes on....and yet here we have nature
Nature still manifesting as the ultimate expression of art in motion
What could be more inspiring?

Thinking of times I spent in Central Park, NYC...

Arrival

He thought how fortunate he was
Luckiest man alive, his conclusion
How could he feel any other way?
He had been to visit hospital
And yet he was in perfect health
A little stressed maybe...yet still fit and healthy
His partner was the reason for the visit
And strangely she was also in perfect health
Even more stress she has been through...yet also fit and healthy
His job had made it impossible to get here sooner
Being halfway above the Atlantic serving drinks saw to that
He came as soon as he could
He found the ward on which his partner resided
They threw their arms around one another and hugged forever
Then he saw her and she stole his heart right there and then
He knew his life would never be the same again
She lay there, eyes struggling to focus on his face
And then she smiled...and he melted
And his partner said gently to him
"Meet your new daughter"

*Inspired by an air steward I met on a New York to London Heathrow
flight...*

To Be Harder Than A Car

Macclesfield, Cheshire, silk its main claim to fame
That and rather poorly playing the beautiful game
Got to feel a little sorry for the Silk Men, as they are known
Doing their best, another game lost, the crowd just groan
Recent years has seen the town centre improved and changed
Looks quite cute these days, yet one thing remains unchanged
The locals born and bred it seems under Cheshire's lucky star
Drive there and you'll see, they think they're harder than a car

Choose any road, doesn't matter back road or high street
The locals at any time by millimetres death they cheat
Deciding to cross the road, off the pavement they go
Never bothering to look or pause a moment to slow
Lived their myself some ten years or more, back in the day
Learning quite quickly to watch for pedestrians gone astray
Yet they never seem to get knocked down, really quite bizarre
Macclesfield, where locals think they're harder than a car

My former home town of Macclesfield

The Wise Kebab Seller

The Ulster bus passed by, confusing jaded minds
We didn't cross water to get here
Only a sign post resplendently announcing a new country
"This area of Scotland has Ulster buses" we are told
If you want to know the truth ask a kebab shop owner apparently
As he enthused about his home town
Selling life there better than any tourist brochure
Purchasing falafels by way of repayment for smiles and bonhomie
Stranraer the town in question
Port looking pretty as the sun goes down
Our wise kebab selling friend told us of the history
Of all the tourist attractions
Castle, museum and waterfront
We've other places to travel to
Always other places to travel too
Some other time…

Light Show

It's the lights that have the greatest impact
Cavalcades of moving colours seem abstract
Fascinated retinal overload in a good sense
Bright, so garishly bright, experientially intense
Observing street art, for it is here made large
Feet propel me, slowly the mind takes charge
Making out pictures amidst beauty chaotic
Thousands also sharing the show hypnotic

Appreciative of coloured lights, pretty much as a rule
And I do adore walking the Illuminations at Blackpool

An appreciation of Blackpool, Lancashire

Penarth

The friendliest of welcomes
Even with my terribly English accent
Not an eye is batted or sly look made
Only smiles and warmth come our way
They can be proud of their town
Spotless it gleams in the mid-day sun
A million jewels reflected on the sea
Or so it seemed on that day...

Welsh coastal town, near Cardiff

Be Seeing You

The lure of the 1960's TV series still attracts
Thousands a year visiting, walking the set
Viewing all the locations, soaking up facts
I guess if that's why you came, it's what you'll get

Yet for us it's different, always having to be different
Clough Williams-Ellis in our opinion genius
The resting place for retired buildings just brilliant
Creating The Village, his vision ingenious

People around us acting out scenes it seems
Barely noticed as architectural styles explored
Utterly randomly scattered, no thought of themes
The more seen, the more deeply adored

Can I also make a Village, please?
Give me some land and buildings I'll save
A vision of kitsch, my own fest of "cheese"
Come invest in my amazing brain wave

My village will have old town halls
Ancient high street shops, Victorian schools
Farms lost to motorways, quaint market stalls
The only rule, like Williams-Ellis, no rules

Portmeirion in Wales, location for the classic TV series The Prisoner

Architectural Gems

It's time for me to raise a glass in cheer
Let's make it orange juice, I don't drink beer
Too often overlooked architectural gems I hold dear
Let's hear it for the great Victorian seaside pier!

I adore piers, I did spend a few years attempting to visit them all, still not quite made it yet...

Starting With Westminster Bridge

It's a good a place to cross as any
London Eye destination of many
But not us, we seek Southbank for sure
It's just other attractions have more allure
Art and creativity our magnetic attraction
Walk past tourists, our vision abstraction
Dali Universe to be our first port of call
Give ourselves all morning taking in it all
She pushes a melting clock it swings with ease
Hanging upon its branch like caught in a breeze
Picasso's in the basement, I wonder if he'd mind?
Playing second fiddle to Dali seems a tad unkind
Prolific Pablo had time to create stunning pottery
We'll buy some ourselves when we win the lottery

Taking our leave, east we leisurely make our way
Stopping taking photos, nourished at riverside café
The Tate invitingly awaits our afternoon pleasure
Home to modernist, abstract, surrealist treasure
Start at the top and work down apparently our plan
Artfully rusty Citroen and genuinely a full trash can
Canvasses painted purest black...even some Andy
Everywhere we look there's more artistic eye candy
After two floors we know we'll have to return

As to gallery shop we decide it's time to adjourn
Exquisite sensory overload happily collectively
Further viewing impossible in any way objectively
As out into daylight we finally decide to venture
Excitedly we already plan our next artistic adventure

Spain Without The Pain

No fish and chips, no trinkets or souvenirs
Not an ice cream shop or any designer beers
No time-share reps, no beautiful people hangin' in bars
Not a euro-anonymous hotel or cheap rental cars

Wild mountain walks overlooking glistening sea
Working town with beautifully functional stone quay
Deserted beach, freshly baked bread from local store
Tourist by-pass the town and Denia we simply adore

Generations

Ribblehead Viaduct…he'd never seen anything so amazing
For hours he stood transfixed, admiringly gazing
How can a work of civil engineering so add to the panorama?
Functional, yet with unparalleled beauty…pure drama

Starting out from Settle early one morning
To catch the steam train he is boarding
Travelling the track and travelling in time
The golden age of railways, pure sublime
His grandfather had worked on this railway
A signal-man, back in his heyday
The journey taking him to all his old haunts
The destinations of all his pleasure jaunts

As he read the Guide he'd bought
He saw how the people had fought
To keep alive this great railway of heritage
Steam fans centre for pilgrimage

His grandfather's words came back to him again
As he felt the almost living power of the train
"Steam gets in your blood and never lets you go,
right from the top of your head, down to your big toe"
And he understood and was full of gratitude
For he had never before got grandfather's attitude
As he sat there watching the landscape flash by

He no longer needed to wonder how or why

Unlike so many others this line got its reprieve
Michael Portillo's decision, what a legacy to leave
Then the hard work truly began
 The volunteers united in their plan

Oh yes…he finally understood all the stories grandfather told
He thought of that gentle, shy man, as his journey did unfold
He realised that he shared completely his passion for steam
He knew what he had to do, volunteer, become part of the team
Two generations of one family, one passed on…one with his life ahead
And a shared great love for spending time in the railway shed
Walk the footsteps his grandfather had trod decades before
And work on the Settle to Carlisle line that they both adore…

Tells the tale of a young man's journey of discovery, learning more about himself and his much missed late grandfather, the action takes place on the Settle to Carlisle railway line

And Write A Poem Or Two In The Process...

Walking the length of Broadway
One afternoon, on a winter's day
White Cliffs Dover to Deal and then back
22 miles said the sign by the track
Through a quagmire in Cheshire rain
Knee deep in mud, no pain no gain
Blackpool seafront gales raging, precipitation
Staying on the ground main preoccupation
Calais ferry cancelled, no room at any inn
Sleeping on the beach, really gotta grin
Playing golf on a hillside, darkness descended
Loosing far more balls than I ever intended
Most uncomfortable mountain bike ever made
Ridden off road, bruises that required first aid
Free-climbing mountains once my great passion
Discovering free-falling not quite the fashion
Yet one passion I will forever seemingly adore
To walk new places, travel and explore...

A True Community

Farming
Growing
Fertile land
Feeding so many

A bus passes through
But only on a Thursday
Eleven on the dot it leaves
To return at three
A chance to visit the metropolis
The big town
Some forty thousand people all told
Sensory overload
Here exist less human souls
Many less
A thousand
Maybe

Village life
Provisions store
It's privately owned
Chain store free zone
Two years ago the post office closed
And with it a century old way of life

A hairdresser
I'm not acquainted with
A beauty therapist
I'm reasonably well acquainted with
The library visits us
On wheels
Twice a month
Literary lifeline

Carl runs the garage
Failing to understand any car made after '95
Suits most of us well
Perfection
Two churches
Take your pick
According to faith

Living by the seasons
Harmony with nature
Working alongside her
A village green
For all the world
Like a thousand jigsaw images

Three pubs await our custom
Each has a darts team
Speaking volumes about our main pastime

Has the English village changed?

Maybe
Well, okay
Yes
Some things remain
Characters
All life going on
Community
Sure, everyone knows your business
May it forever remain
A true community

*I have experienced life in several English villages and may they exist
forever...evolving, yet remaining constant*

A Tale of Two Trains

Up to one hundred and twenty-five miles an hour they say
Free wi-fi, charge your phone as you travel on your way
Streamlined Pendolino trains miracle of this hi-tech existence
Kick back, have a coffee, you won't feel the distance
Doors open, another town before us can wait no more
In my mind I travel back, right back to glorious days of yore

Up to one hundred and twenty-six miles an hour records say
At the helm driver Joe Duddington alongside fireman Bray
Streamlined Mallard to Sir Nigel Gresley owed its existence
Faster and faster she went over the measured distance
The record still holds, and probably will for ever more
She survives, archaic reminder of those glorious days of yore

It seems nothing is new, wonderful though modern Pendolino trains are,
in 1938 steam could match it for speed (if not eco-friendliness)

The Jacket

Her most treasured possession
Fraying
Veritably threadbare
Once brown
Now no longer
Original colour faded out
Existing only in memory
As he does now
Grandpops
Her adored Grandpops

Three years since he passed away
His jacket
The one he wore come rain or shine
Became hers
Only hers
And the emotions
Which came with it
She wore it every day
His jacket
Come rain or shine
He somehow feeling closer
Protecting her even now
As he once had

What now?
As the jacket
His jacket
Borrowed from him
On permanent loan
Now worn by her
Gently wears out
She cries
Tears of despair
What now?
No amount of cleaning
Of repairing
Patching up
Can save it
Things wear out
Memories don't
What now?

A suggestion arrives from afar
Grandpops lives in you
In those treasured times
His words of love
Of humour
His jacket
Your jacket
The symbol
Of all he was
Find an exact replica
Have one made if needs be

Like when it was new
When Grandpops wore it the first time
It's the remembrance
Deep inside
Your new jacket
Worn
In honour of his jacket
It will still hold the memories
Every single one of them

New jacket
Same old warmth

So she did
And it does
Comforts her
This new jacket
Exactly like before
Worn with love

What of Grandpops old jacket?
Framed, it hangs in her den
She smiles up at it
And dances a happy dance
Just as she did with Grandpops
So many times
Wearing her
His jacket

Nature Freely Gives

Jack In The Green awakens from his slumber
Spring is upon us, nature in all her wonder
Gaze in awe of rebirth, renewal, fertility
Stood deep in the forest, deep within tranquillity

Robin Goodfellow his mischief to perform
Souring milk, trampling crop circles from fields of corn
Tripping those who into the green wood unwary tread
Laughing, yet another traveller away from path he led

Puck so much more than a Midsummer Night's Dream
Shakespeare drawing upon history, the arcane, unseen
Trickster of faery folk, denizen of mischievous games and fun
Beware, if he enchants you, from those woods you'll never run

Herne the Hunter now be wary here, take heed
Horns upon his head, the wildest wild hunt he leads
Terrified peasants flee from upon his path
Lest they feel the full forth of his awful wrath

Robin Hood, legend tells many tales of his noble deeds
Taking only from rich, to the poor sharing his proceeds
Did he exist, the debate lingers on, I think live he once must
With his merry band, close to nature, righting the unjust

The Green Man, guardian of all that truly matters
Without the woods, forest, trees, our ecosystem shatters
Summer sun to winter's frozen whitest beauty
He oversees it all, such is The Green Man's duty

Of all these characters who's stories I shared this day
A common thread exists and I feel compelled to say
Treasure the green wood, as all nature freely gives
Knowing any less than that is to hardly even live

These faery folk, Robin Hood and The Green Man have come down to us from ancient ballad and poetry writers, that these stories have survived down through millennia only serves to underline their continued relevance and importance to us in this time

Be Beautiful...

It's all around if we open our eyes to see
Today I saw a gorgeous tree
Growing out of an old crumbling wall
There lies beauty
It's everywhere around
And it costs nothing

I am giving beauty the chance it deserves

I'm What's His Face

The presenting of many a poetic radio show
Doesn't ensure recognition wherever I go
Live performances to varied venues I travel
An hour or two of attention as poetic tales unravel
Television interviews thrust me into the spotlight
Talking of poems and the other words I write
Why The Quantum Poet invariably they ask
TV friendly sound-bites becoming my main task
Next happens probingly enquiring of my aspirations
Shortly followed by wishing to know my inspirations
I say hip hop and rap are poetry, they usually agree
How long have I been writing and what next for me?
A legacy for future generations I assert is crucial
And telling how to buy my books especially useful
So passes by another fifteen or thirty minutes of fame
Don't get me wrong I love appearing on TV all the same
Especially when the supermarket queue I later grace
As an inquisitive soul asks "Aren't you what's his face?"

What it is like being recognised and yet apparently not quite able to be placed, although I have happily had people come up to me in a mall to recite their poetry and it is lovely, I always give them some of my attention and time

The Drawer in the Mine

He a drawer deep underground
A driver of ponies
Of small stature
Perfectly suited to task
His job
Other men toiling
Inching forward each day
Filling tubs with black gold
Coal to fuel
Keeping the wheels of industry turning
The drawer, Robert Hampson his name
Subterranean friend to pit ponies
Moving impossibly heavy loads
Making way for yet more back-breaking work
And yet it was his destiny
All he knew
He didn't have to dig like so many
His father and grandfather before him
They had been drawers
Knowing horses right there in his blood
His genes
Soon he would leave the mine
New experiences
Life always changes
The unexpected happens
Yet for his time

Deep in the mine
He was happy

A drawer used to be responsible for transporting coal from the face to the surface. This is part of the story of my own great grandfather, for more of his tale and to see where he went next, have a look at the poem Boots 2 in my book The Lancashire Poems

Have a Good Day, Mr Magpie

La Gazza Ladra, Rossini gave us an opera
The Thieving Magpie his choice of drama
Cunning avian immortalized by nursery rhyme
One for what was it? The magpie's next crime?
This Al Capone of flight, gangster bird, larger than life
Intelligence is here, quick thinking, sharper than a knife
Other birds shun it, does it feel or even care?
All I know when spotted by me unless in a pair
A solitary magpie always evokes the same response
A salute from me and quickly muttered once
"Hello Mr Magpie, how's your wife and kids?"
Any other words superstition strictly forbids
The curse now suitably broken yet again
Dignity I can attempt to somehow regain

I have wanted to write of magpies for a while and yes, I really do go through all that performance when I spot a solitary one

The Old Straight Track

The greenest valley spread far and wide
Slowly settlement starts on either side
Bronze age people, eventually two villages grew
Looking from a distance at one another, what next to do?
Great plans are conceived, as elders confer to discuss
To be better able to trade, a track we'll make between us
The Dodman by description, early surveyor of the land
Making sure the track was straight by his own fair hand
And straight for sure it became, shortest route attainable
Two villages connected in peace, with a bond unbreakable
Trading, marrying with their neighbours in the valley
A thousand years or more co-existing quite happily

An invasion, alien ways, ruled by another hand
Roman legions taking over exactly as planned
The people settled eventually, amicable existence
Alongside the Romans, yet still kept their distance
Across the valley, the villas and bathhouses grew
Centurions marched the old straight track anew
The gromatici, Roman surveyor, got a commendation
Made the track their own through their time of occupation

Middle ages two villages either side of the valley floor
People travelled on horse, just as on foot once before
Taken for granted, the old track, as history unfolded
The industrial revolution next upon the scene exploded

A great engineer had a plan, Brunel by name
Unite this land together and do it by train
Our valley he viewed, surveyed and found it good
We'll lay track here, using the old route we should
Two villages either side of the valley, connected by steam
Twenty minutes' journey must have seemed like a dream
A hundred years the villages prospered, became rich
Track surviving two wars, trains continued without a hitch

1960's the railways needed to profit, pay their way
Dr Beeching tasked to make it happen, the final say
Brutally, with logic his tool, he closed stations and lines
To the old straight track the end, it seems had come the time
Two villages either side of the valley far and wide
No longer connected, their togetherness just died
Three thousand years of harmony gone in a flash
Community sacrificed over the gods of hard cash
The old route overgrown, for the first time unused
What now, to disappear forever, train track removed

Twenty first century begins, looking forward at the past
A local Council meeting and a question finally asked
"let's make a footpath, across the valley floor
Connect the two villages once again, like before"
It came to pass, the way cleared, gravel lain
A new era, new time, the old track born again
Along the way picking up a national tourism award
Ten years it's been open, it's future now assured
Two villages, countless generations been and gone

Yet all have enjoyed the old straight track to walk upon

Never Meet Your Heroes

Melting clocks
The memory persists
A moment of genius
Pure sublime
Symbolism
And yet so much more
Inspired so many childish artistic endeavours
My tentative ventures into art
Paint
Immortalized in my paint
Still the memory persists
Drawing me in
To see
Needing to see
Reach out into the painting
What was the artist feeling?
Could I feel it too?
Compelled to witness first hand
And I did
Tiny in proportion
This giant of influence
In the gallery
Having it to myself
Quiet time of the day
Stood
Studying

Stunned
And I felt
Well
Less impressed now
Oddly considerably less impressed

In 2006 I travelled to The Museum of Modern Art in New York to fulfil a childhood dream to see Dali's The Persistence of Memory and found myself slightly underwhelmed, although I did love discovering Van Gogh - he hadn't been lost, I just never really noticed his work before!

The Dancers of Life

Sticks clash together as the bells ring
Heralding Centuries old rites of spring
Morris Men dancing in each season
Each well-rehearsed step for a reason
The fiddle player keeping with tradition
Lending the dance for all his rhythm
Denizen of all things beauteous and green
The village has chosen The May Queen
Morris Men dancing good harvest to bring
Then the fool is crowned the misrule King
The green wood, the field ripe with corn
From winter's deathly hold, spring is reborn
Every jig performed, every "hey" and every dance
If you be lucky enough to watch them perchance
Be sure to applaud and treat them with respect
They do this for all of us, mother nature to protect

In market square or village green the dance goes on
Through countless generations and the dance goes on
Right across this fairest land forever the dance goes on

The first written record of Morris Men dates back six centuries and the tradition was already ancient even then

The Shaman in the Park

He walks as he chants, feeling the grass beneath his feet
Smiling inwardly, he knows who he came here to meet
Sacred sounds reverberate, into air and within the ground
Soon it happens, by him they swoop, begin to fly around
Warmer weather is here, swallows confirming this
As by fractions of a centimetre our shaman they miss
Feeling his energy, chanting he continues, projecting love
Dancing aerially around him, they skim his arms held above
Then the spell is broken, a curious dog barks its presence
Birds flee, the shaman gives thanks and returns to the present

A story of your poet and his communication with nature, in this case
perhaps twenty or so swallows recently returned to these shores to enjoy
the summer warmth

Linger a Little Longer

Linger a little longer in our home
Before once again you must roam
Tell us of your travellers' tales
Spare us none of the details

Stay with us, more precious stories
Of strangest lands and territories
Those desert sunsets you bore witness
Your need to go when you feel listless

Yet talk some more and lay down here
Of more adventures we long to hear
The silk route taken and the olive trail
Of every mountain you had to scale

Be with us for a little more time
Share our food, drink our wine
Regale us with happy song and dance
Full of mystery and a little romance

Rest awhile our dearest friend
We know to journeys you must attend
Linger a little longer with us right here
For all too soon you will disappear

The story of an adventurous friend who is absolutely compelled to travel, new horizons constantly call her

Connected Through Time and Sword

PART ONE

No more the battlefield for him
No more kill or be killed
A life he had known since he cared to remember
Cast aside
As he now casts aside the tools of death

He makes his way
Avenue of standing stones he knows so well
Island in the lake his destination
Sacred place of ritual
Across timber walkway he crosses

His brother had died by the sword
Fallen in battle like so many
He felt world weary
Once his father had fallen also
He felt oh so world weary

His finest bronze sword in his hand
Like so many times before
This time the reason differed
This time he came in peace

To make peace

Raising his sword high above his head
His shout heard all across the valley
"Goddess take my sword
in peace I choose to live!"
Casting it into the lake

He watched for a while
Ripples settling on the water
Then calmness, as he now felt inside
Taking his leave of that place
And his former life

PART TWO

He sought to understand
This man of learning
Professorship was one thing
Hands-on his eternal passion
Archaeology means digging

This site drew him
Like moth to flame
Coursing deep through his blood
Feeling kinship to this place
To know more

Our ancestors, his ancestors
Ancient landscape he could read
The lake still seen in his mind's eye
Now long silted up
Mound signified the island

Experience told him Bronze Age
He felt sure
Excavation
Reaching into the past
A glimpse into lives long gone

And then they found it
Dirt encrusted it saw daylight once again
Even after all these years
All those digs
He felt the familiar thrill

Later, cleaned and preserved
This legacy from another time
Was it ritual?
Cast into the water as sacrifice?
He sat in quiet contemplation

Then suddenly it overwhelmed him
Compelled to hold the sword
Feeling deep into the past
Through this sword…his ancestor spoke
And he saw and he understood

Bodging in the Woods

A crafting bodger by trade is he
Residing in the woods he be
By the seasons he lives
Using what nature gives
Feeling every tree in the wood
Bodging runs deep in his blood
Spindles for chairs he makes
Only what he needs he takes
Coppicing his forest friends
The circles of life never ends
Spending his days productively
Furniture he crafts lovingly
Beauty in every knot, every joint
No nails or screws is the point
For here we have true art
Words alone cannot impart
Watch the bodger creating
His man powered lathe rotating
By chisel and saw, truly hand made
For his labours he is duly well paid
Yet for him the money matters not
It's about living here, in this spot
In touch with the past, nary a machine
At one with the woods and all that is green

Bodgers are traditional craftsmen and women who live in the woods, expertly taking care of it and using only what they need to make their beautifully rustic wooden items. They go back far into antiquity. Here in England there are still a handful of people carrying on the trade, their creations are highly sought after and prized

Finding Himself in Nature

Deep in the heart of the forest
He lingers a moment to rest
He knows well his destination
Two hours meander his estimation
Finding the oldest tree of all, he hesitates
Sat, leant against the trunk he meditates

High within the mountain peaks
Within himself answers he seeks
All the world below somewhere
Quietly he finds his spot up there
Sheltered by cairn, thoughts he elevates
Gale rages all around as he meditates

Waves roar as they crash upon beach
Yet he's here some wisdom to reach
Upon his rock facing the wildest sea
Spray washed, alive he feels such empathy
As once again he enters altered states
In the heart of the storm, he meditates

Natural wonder he found all around
Emanating from deep within the ground
Carried on the wind, the rain and snow
Seeking answers in caves or plateau
Whatever journey he undertakes

Wherever he goes, he meditates

I have meditated since my teenage years (a little while ago) and although I love to meditate on trains, my preferred location is always within nature

Fogou

Subterranean enigma the enduring mystery
Historians the use for which no two can agree
For storing grain, defences from attack or weather
Intuition speaks of a different role altogether

The wise man or woman, shaman of the clan
Their incantations and spells right there began
Entering the darkness of the fogou
These iron age magicians all knew
Deep within the womb of mother earth
Rituals of plentiful harvest were given birth
Fertility of the land ensured by their wisdoms
Protecting the people, chiefs and their kingdoms
Strange incantations long lost to the modern ear
Yet spend time in the fogou you might just hear
Words from aeons past travelling through time
A warning for us to take heed of their sign
To cherish this planet, feel how she lives
Taking from her only that she freely gives

*A fogou (pronounced foo-goo) is man-made subterranean iron-age cave
systems most famously found in Cornwall, England, yet also seen in
other places. Their precise use remains a mystery, ancient grain particles
were found in archaeological digs, leading some to think they were for
storage, my theory is these were offerings made to ensure a good harvest*

Acting Upon a Dream

A vision of another time
Feeling the landscape
Reaching into the past
Mineral rich
Quarry his location
Seeking
Seeking to communicate
Follow his intuition
Off the well walked track
Reading the ground
With closed eyes, he sees
And walks with purpose
Yes, it is just as he saw
Yes!

Hidden under long grass
This hollowed out depression
He drops to the ground
Hands feeling, seeing
As he knew it would be
This ancient smelting place
Suddenly his fingers touch something
Partly buried
Prising his prize from the Earth
Copper ore
Pure copper ore

What he came here for
Long thought long gone
He had a dream
Acted upon

This piece of rock
His gift
It is well travelled
Two continents it has visited
Held in such esteem
Treasured
It goes with him
Protective talisman
Or perhaps taliswoman
Copper of the goddess
She watches over him

I travelled to a long disused quarry, after I saw it in a dream and found the small piece of pure copper ore mentioned in this poem. It has remained my constant companion for nearly two decades

Turner Surprise

Our pilgrimage in honour of his art
To nourish the soul, culture impart
Locations as our schedule can accommodate
Mentally travelling back in time to appreciate
Centuries on would he recognise the views?
Were he to stand here now, wearing our shoes
Genius of a bygone age, his legacy lives right on
A prize named after him, this artistic paragon
Wandering and wondering continued our quest
Finally overlooking the river, we linger to rest
And it happens, we look at one another, happy tears we cry
Laid out before us, the view he saw, and above a Turner sky

*A tribute to the painter J.M.W Turner, famous for his incredible skies
and the view he frequently painted of The River Thames from Richmond
Hill*

The River and The Sea

A canoe launches into shallowest water
All but a stream
High in the mountains
Forward motion begins
Avoiding rocks
Patiently progress is made
Slowly yet surely
Widening and then
In an instant transformed
A cacophony of noise fills his ears
Rapids!
With long-won skill, he traverses
Shooting onwards
Summersaulting
Yet in control
Then calm returns
First signs of civilization
Ducks loudly announce their surprise
This alien intruder into their world
People fish along the banks
He steers a course away from their lines
Some wave hello
Others glare as his wake disturbs the fish
The town is reached
Graffiti he passes
Some is art made loud

Others proclaim allegiance to sports teams
Or unknown gangs
Two worlds co-exist here
Busy road and once busy river
Parallel
All activity going on
The people seemingly on fast-forward
Few spare him attention
As he breathes traffic pollution
Road left behind as a troubled memory
Into the park
Children wave
Raised paddle in salute
Smiling faces
Running along the banks
Then he's gone
Park also left behind
Other vessels use this river now
Pleasure boats, luxurious yachts
Gracing the harbour
His canoe tiny amongst the hustle and bustle
Four hours his journey
Travelling with the river
Today she co-operated
Let him pass in peace
He feels even tinier now
As into the sea he paddles
And he never felt so alive
He follows the coastline

Secluded bay
Far from people
Towering cliffs behind him
Canoe dragged upon the beach
Laying in the mid-day sun
Eating at last
Exhausted
Yet at peace

An adventure following the call of the river from the mountains all the way to harbour and then sea

Tales to Tell

Fine jester in the court of noble king
Telling his stories in songs to sing
If he didn't please, he'd lose his head
Which would leave him feeling pretty dead

Music hall orator his tales shared
Before his audience his soul he bared
Needing to be fit, fast on his legs
If unliked he'd be pelted with eggs

Before them stood the poet tall
In tradition of jester and music hall
Hoping his audience wowed and awed
Then at the end they might just applaud

*My life as a twenty first century poetic story-teller is rather less fraught
with the dangers some of my predecessors had to endure*

Mandolino

Smiling people gather round
Drawn by the beautiful sound
Across all of Europe and Africa
Italy, England across to Croatia
Keeping a tradition of millennia past
Reaching hearts in a way unsurpassed
Folk tunes or jazz it doesn't matter which
Such is the power it possesses to bewitch
As the music unfolds touching all deep within
The playing of a master of the mandolin

Versions of a mandolin-like instrument have been played for over a thousand years, this poem is dedicated to the brilliant Chris Leslie, multi-instrumentalist and a fine exponent of the instrument in question

The Water Diviners

Treading the fields with his hazel twig
Showing farmers exactly where to dig
Parched crops wilting as far as eyes can see
Water hidden, over there, by the old yew tree
The water diviner struck liquid gold once again
A well sunk, the crops lifeblood soon to regain
Year after year, the farmer's gratitude enough
Brian the village legend always did his stuff

Is water divining passed on through generations?
There is one other, dowsing myriads of applications
Brian is his Uncle and yet his own path taken
Dowsing energy within the earth to awaken
Another time, another place, he explored his capability
His best-selling book on dowsing enhanced his credibility
Having read his words, Uncle Brian nodded sagely
This wise man's approval mattered to him greatly

Two men, both of the Earth, doing their divining thing
Hazel twig, rods or pendulum in their hands swing
Two generations united in a common purpose, a goal
Helping others selflessly, find water, go dig a hole

Water diving or dowsing goes back far into the mists of time and to many is still the best way to locate water in drought ridden country areas.

Check out my own best-selling book Unlock Your Life with Pendulum Dowsing if you would like to know more (shameless plug by your poet!)

Farming Through Time

He remembers his great grandfather
Wisdom etched in all the lines creasing his face
He said
"we don't own this land, we look after it for our sons and the sons
of our sons"
And this is how history unfolded
Down through countless generations
His own father before him
Grandad
Right back
The farm
Cared for
Nurtured
By those with the same surname
Passed down once again
Unbroken traditions
Five centuries of history
He feels it right there
In his blood
Walking this land of his ancestors
He feels it through the soles of his boots
Love for the soil
This place he cares for
Nurtured and farmed
Growing crops to feed the people
One day he will pass it on

He feels proud
The bloodline continues
The future assured
One day he knows
His daughter will take over

An appreciation of those growers of the crops which feed us, farmers are not always given the respect they deserve and yet they provide for all of us

Island of My Mind

I would look from my window yonder
Untamed nature
Wild
Waves crashing upon beach
Heart of winter
Gales pounding
Residing here
Pioneering buccaneer
Safe in my sanctuary

Seasons change

I would share this transient place
My island
Wild
Waves lap gently upon beach
Heart of summer
Warming breeze
Growing here
Deeply see and hear
Safe in my paradise

My dream to live on a smallish island, living by the seasons, acceptant of
the extremes nature freely gives and feeling so creatively free in the
process in return

Embracing Nature, Only Natural

PART ONE

Urban environment
Disassociated from nature
Only nature encountered
A green blur
Seen from car or train windows
Rushing on by
Us humans have a deep
You could call it primeval
Existing right there in our DNA
Connection to nature
Our nature to be found
Within nature
Zombie-like existence
Living a half life
All too disconnected from nature
Truly wild areas
Feared
Somewhere to be scared of
Living 24/7 in completely artificial environments
Killing creativity
Deadening intuition
Then comes the need
Real nature is encountered

Take some of this artificial Comfort Zone out there as well…

PART TWO

And I see them
Those walking deep within ancient tranquil forest
Climbing high upon a mountain
Canoeing upon tranquil river
Headphones on
Plugged into music
Maybe I miss out here?
My music collection stays at home
Rather than joining me on walks
In nature
Parallels drawn in my mind
Painted in words
A concert
Favourite band or symphony
Wearing a motorbike crash helmet
Ensuring only half the experience
Coming away disappointed
What was all the fuss about?
Sensory underload

PART THREE

To exercise in nature
First choice every time
Walking or running

Tai chi or meditating
Purest natural setting
Far from only taking exercise
Oh, such more than ever taking exercise
Inspirational
On every level
My best ideas
Poetry or life
How often one and the same
Those ground-breaking ideas
Popped into my head
As they usually do
Way out in the wilderness
Or in the middle of deserted ancient Neolithic site
And very rarely in the middle of a busy city...

Large proportions of the populous have never been so disconnected from nature, if I might be so bold as to make a suggestion? If you are already appreciative of nature, and as you are reading this collection I have the inkling you might be, please take your friends or family members who haven't yet noticed the wonderful natural wonders going on right now and allow them to see for themselves, let your enthusiasm enthuse them

Today in this 21st Century

Today I pull up the drawbridge
My domain
My castle
None may enter

Today I go to the mountain
My niche
My cave
None may find me

Today I commune with nature
My forest
My seashore
None may follow

Today I bid adieu for a while
My freedom
My retreat
None may know

The simpler life our ancestors knew...

So Many Words

Words
Words
Words
So many words
So many words
So many words
Words of threat
Words of bullying
Words of thoughtlessness
Words can crush any potential

Words
Words
Words
So many words
So many words
So many words
Words of encouragement
Words of support
Words to lend a Loving hand
Words can move any mountain

Elements of Inspiration

Taking my inspiration from the green green wood
Home to Herne the Hunter and good Robin Hood
Sunlight sparkling through the canopy of trees
Botanical ecosystem living in harmony with ease
A symphony of nature provided by operatic birdsong
Natural balance perfecting, every creature does belong

Taking my inspiration from the mountain top
Rising high into the sky like it will never stop
The sunset transcending anything seen before
Reflected in the mirrored lake on the valley floor
Strongest winds attempting to dislodge me to a fall
High upon the mountain, sitting taking in it all

Taking my inspiration from the blue seashore
Sat upon the beach as the tide comes ashore
The sun transforms water as a million diamonds
Mesmerizing waves roaring in their guidance
Seagulls diving in and out of the white foam
Secluded bay far from people, for once truly alone

Remembering these wondrous places in my mind
Feeling gratitude mixed with inner peace combined
Pondering magical appreciating freely given beauty
To stand and gaze in awe at all of nature's booty
Look around and within, cherish all Earth has to give

Knowing any less than that is to only partially live

Look to nature…on one hand an eco-friendly poetic journey and then again perhaps it's about our inner path…

The Dawning of Understanding

So many feel the need to fight
Living life without inner light
Why do so many appal
Simple fact that Love is all
My desire all lost souls see
Potential for all they can be
Life make of what we will
Finding our own truths until
Our future to be shaping, moulding
Parallel with our learning unfolding
Emotional balance only natural
Energy, happiness becomes factual
Never was anyone else to blame
Personal responsibility to reclaim
Within us all, now expanding
The dawning of understanding

A Gift to You

Some people say that they cannot use the power of their mind,
they say it's impossible to vision anything
Nothing to inspire them, nothing deep inside for them to seek,
nothing to make their heart and soul sing
Think of a beautiful tropical island looking like paradise on Earth,
palm trees gently sway in the breeze
The healing warmth of the sun as it kisses lightly upon your skin,
relaxing for once enjoying being at total ease
Walking barefoot making virgin footprints in the hot sand, feeling
it coming up between your toes
Beautiful birdsong fills the air as the waves wash gently, scents
from exotic flowers fill your nose

*A meditation focus...visit "my" tropical island any time you like...relax
and enjoy*

Ancestors

Are we happier than our ancient ancestors were?
Seems more stressed if we dare to compare?
Simpler lives close to nature they did lead
These days all the pressure is to succeed
Alien to our ancestors, their life by the seasons
Are we unhappy? Look within for the reasons
Our connection to the Earth replaced by online life
News channels telling tales of trouble and strife
Reclaim our birth-right our DNA from the past
Waits right these inside us, all wisdom amassed
Unlock ourselves, discover first hand
Journey within…reconnect to the land
Harmony and truths eternal to deliver
Work at no longer pushing the river
To be happier like our ancestors were
Less stress when we care to compare

Our ancestors are right there waiting to guide us if we allow them…

A Healing For Gaia

Arbor Low Stone Circle a new day is dawning
Transcendent sunrise welcomes in the morning
Sunshine warming us and the dew laden ground
At one with nature we are chanting sacred sound
Resonating with the landscape, the stones, at last
Through our ancestor's legacy reaching into the past
Vibrations of aeons locked within the circular aspect
There is wisdom here for those affording due respect
We're feeling small here, yet at once interconnected
Seeking nothing for us, only healing for Gaia effected
Help us open the eyes of those unable to yet see
Protect this Earth in all her magnificent glory
Denizens of the stones you revered this sacred land
Let us together take the unenlightened by the hand
Respect one another and this Earth on which we live
Seeking not for themselves but to rather freely give
Harmony in every thought, peace within reactions
Gentleness in words, Love projected in all actions

Beautiful Garden

Anne Hathaway's cottage stands awaiting our pleasure
Yet the gardens are divine in the midday sun
An arbour invites lingering for our further leisure
Playing word games Rose of Eros, Orange of No Rage
Would Anne Hathaway recognise this garden now?
Would "he" write a sonnet sat right where we are?
If "he" did then we can certainly understand how
Peaceful contemplation against a chorus of birdsong
Most beautiful dragonfly you ever did see
Hummingly seemingly also taking in the view
As it gently decides to land there on my left knee
The spell is broken as the latest house tour ends
People spill into garden invading our space once more
What we found there will always stay with us
Love in harmony with nature, creates all we adore

A visit to Stratford-upon-Avon...another poem written on the banks of the Avon...like so many times before...

Oneness

Please help open my mind
Rationality limits potential
Quieten pointless ponderings
Let my mind be free
A thousand random thoughts vie for attention
Only the chatter of mundaneness
Never did mean anything
Time for a new chapter
Overdue awakening within
Intuition then inner knowing
To be still from inside out
To listen to nothing
Calmness permeates
At last…

Intuition or gut instinct call it what you may…even spirit…attune to it and it will guide you

To the Mountain to Freedom

She had journeyed far from the valley below
Through many trials compelled to undergo
Ascent the hardest choice and yet no choice
Listening as she had to her own inner voice
Her focus, her life spent climbing upwards
Often two steps forward, one backwards
Determinedly she continued her endless quest
Grateful to know the mountain, deeply blessed
Looking back she sees obstacles now long gone
She knew they would pass if she only pushed on
Trials and tribulations tested if she's faint hearted
Immeasurable distance from where she started
Her ascent to the summit, her own path taken
One dimensional existence long since forsaken
And yet the path now also seems to be gone
She pondered with an open mind thereupon
Panic and worry having long since been banished
Looking back every obstacle has now also vanished
Considering her journey in her own minds eye
Dawning realisation hit her, now she could FLY!

Testing Times – To Walk the Talk

Duplicity bringing decisions to make
Is our still point true or horribly fake?
Acts of others testing our poise
Full of anger, making some noise
Ahhh turn away or get involved?
Situations needing to be resolved
Once upon a time perhaps pro-action?
Testing times now, so what reaction?
Wasted energy with pointless futility?
Be angry as well, words of hostility?
Better to focus on our own pathway
Personal journey now well underway
Being prepared to lower our reactions
For the sake of such un-evolved actions
How we reflecting how we feel inside
Anger washes over us, brushed aside
Those seeking to grow will always encounter
People wanting bring us onto their downer
Needing a way of keeping our calmness
A way of dealing with negative darkness
Why not just smile and peacefully say
"I send you love and have a good day!"

Eyes Open Wide

With purest open heart
Negativity now depart
In beauty walking
Inner voice talking
Cleansed, whole
Mind, body, soul
Harmonious living
Smiles easily giving
Complete inside
Eyes open wide
Still point that is sought
All actions all thought
Transformation undergo
To understand, to know
Truly deeply fathom
Love in every atom…

Shhh

So many people busy talking at us
Aggressively vocalising what they discuss
Try with great passion to change our mind
Often using insults or expressions unkind
Loudly to make us see their point of view
Failing to listen, through their hullabaloo

Shhh...Listen to the silence...

Oranges to Teach us All

The meaning of orange
The colour of no rage
Hidden inside orange
Lays waiting no rage
Oh mysterious orange
Being free from rage
Wear the shirt orange
Living a life of no rage
Ever enough orange?
Being free from rage
Orangey is the orange
No rage is all the rage
Hail the happy orange
The essence of no rage

Latent wisdom within this most poetically challenging of words...

The Serene Moon

The Moon looked down upon the dwellers in the city
Illuminated silent observer casting light
People going about their life with such intense intent
What lesson do you teach oh beautiful serene moon?
Your light existing only as a reflection from the sun
With your dark side so well hidden

Just as we walk this earth
Illuminated by a higher force
Duality constantly at play
Look upwards in the clear night
Reminder to all to shine
Reflecting brightly our beautiful serene us of us…

Yin -Yang, another in my series of Moon Poems

Global Island

Sark, idyllic island without a single car
Anywhere you'd wish to go, is not so far
A relaxing life, taken at a much slower pace
Everyone friendly, it's just that kind of place
Always having time for a chilled conversation
Local's attitude to life, like one long vacation
Sure they work, often hard, yet never a chore
They see it as adding to the community they adore

Seems about perfect to me, wonder if you agree?
So perfect in fact I'd like to make a heartfelt plea
Sark in the Channel Islands microcosmic role model
Scale up their template across the Earth to remodel
New focuses, new priorities, new ways of being
From the treadmill existence everyone be freeing
Life about happiness, living love, global community
Every nation as one, existing in perfect unity…

A beautiful Channel Island helped inspire these words

Dreams

The plumber dreamt of being a musician
The musician dreamt of being a magician
The magician dreamt of being a florist
The florist dreamt of being a chemist
The chemist dreamt of being a judge
The judge dreamt of making fudge

Got to make all those dreams come true
Take action, do it now, it's down to you

The mechanic dreamt of being a meteorologist
The meteorologist dreamt of being a sociologist
The sociologist dreamt of being a train driver
The train driver dreamt of being a deep sea diver
The deep sea diver dreamt of being a psychiatrist
The psychiatrist dreamt of being a unicyclist

Got to make all those dreams come true
Take action, do it now, it's down to you

The grandmother dreamt of being at University
The student dreamt of being at sea
The sailor dreamt of being at home
The sailor's wife felt oh so alone
The loner made a wish to the power's above
Please let me find my only one true love

Got to make all those dreams come true
Take action, do it now, it's down to you

How many of us follow our dreams? Took me a while to get there...I hope it takes you less time

Endless Possibilities

Confidence comes from self-knowing
Knowing is to journey within
Within is the source of all wisdom
Wisdom is to truly master life
Life is about self-knowing
Knowing oneself is growing
Growing is the true path
Paths all lead to inner wisdom
Wisdom is an acceptance
Acceptance is to know oneself
Oneself the true source of knowing
Knowing yet never knowing all
All we exist for is growing
Growing onwards mastering life
Life needing to manifest wisdom
Wisdom knowing eternally growing
Forever...

Paradoxically

21st Century Vegan

Choices we make as we face each day
Which clothes to wear, cash or card to pay
What to eat, what to drink, where to travel
Look around reality and see it all unravel
One choice I made to embrace veganism
Now dining out can cause a big schism
Animal products I avoid in entirety
Kinda out of step with the rest of society
"But what do you eat?" I so often hear
Let me tell you one more time, make it quite clear
Nothing that could cause needless harm
That come from rivers or lives on a farm
Avoiding any animal ingredient
I consider most expedient
This story is all about me
My choice to live cruelty free

Trust in You

What is false and what is real?
Can we really trust the way we feel?
Are perceptions the ultimate illusions?
Our minds creating the greatest delusions?
Books partially helping in growing
Better attuned to our inner knowing
Re-learning all knowledge once we knew
The energy of pure love to eternally renew

Anti-war requires a war to exist
Pro-peace and war will desist...

Inspiration in a Rose

Inspiration…where to seek pure inspiration?
That innermost creative beauteous elation
Living the urban life and wondering how
Is inner connection possible here and now?
Walking these city streets looking around
It's alive in the buildings, people and sound
Yet here is nature, she never quite goes
Find yourself a park and go smell a rose

Doesn't matter which variety of rose …just find one that has a nice fragrance

Zen – Spiritual Tea

In order to make good tea
First you need the water
Then add the tea
And leave to brew
The combination greater
Than the sum of its parts
Without the tea
All you end up
Is unfulfilled

In order to evolve, grow
First you need the desire
Then add the will
And leave to brew
The combination greater
Than the sum of its parts
Without the will
All you end up
Is unfulfilled

A Non Spiritual, Spiritual Story

Fragrant tea rose
Butterfly on the nose
Warmth of the sun
Cinnamon sticky bun
Hot spicy ginger tea
Bench looking out to sea
Sole fell off my shoe
Stick it back on with glue
Sunflower bumble bee
Ferryman pay the fee
Fragrances sweet pea
Externalized inner chi
Question all we see
Rejecting or agree
Find our way home
Imprinted genome
All yew trees know
The way to grow
Immortality there within
Our spiritual arboreal twin
Locked deep in our DNA
We'll understand some day
Timing perfect alignment
The body most magnificent

Limitation forever ended
The key to being ascended

Yew trees and humans share a common neuropeptide, the trigger for
longevity

City Life – Follow Your Bliss

His friends thought what a pity
Abandoning his job in the city
They judged him to be quite mad
Early mid-life crisis, how sad

Next he distributed some of his wealth
Considered it essential for good health
Trinkets of a life he'd turned away from
And pretty soon he will also be long gone

A Scottish island to be his new home
Clean air, wildness, freedom to roam
He'll craft arty things from driftwood
His life harmonized natural and good

His inner voice he could no longer ignore
Happiness his reality like never before
A simpler new life and his soul is at ease
To inner bliss and contentment, he has the keys

Sometimes he ponders all the wasted years
All the deals he did; blood, sweat and tears
"Life carries on there, they won't think of me
My decision to seek big skies and blue sea"

From his window every season looks pretty
Winters are harsh, but then so is the city
If they're happy in the city, he's glad they are
For himself he's grateful he's come so far...

Walking away from one reality for something more real to the man in this tale...

Magic Gems

Rock Crystal of purest energy
Smoky Quartz creating good chi
Amethyst powerful healer
Apache Tear karmic revealer
Rose Quartz the love stone
Carnelian "in the zone"
Tigereye Gold attracts wealth
Malachite the aid to health
Amazonite for lucky days
Sunstone sunshine rays
Bloodstone the blood tonic
Snowflake Obsidian life harmonic
Moonstone sweet dreams
Black Obsidian reveals unseen
Pink Agate have a good rest
Flourite for passing a test
Blue Obsidian wish making
Green Jade for stomach aching
Blue Howlite pure happiness
Amber for financial success
Orange Calcite much laughter
Rainbow Moonstone happy ever after…

Bring some crystals into your life…

Seasons Of Reasons

The whole forest awakens into Spring
Buds and leaves freshly formed on trees
Bluebells carpet the ground
Soon, very soon all life reborn
In anticipation of Summer

Summer sun a forest resplendent
Harmonic balance of existence
Birds share their songs generously
Warmth filters through canopies of branches
And it seems so long 'til Autumn

Autumn brings a gentle winding down
Scenery thrills in red, gold and green
A thousand scents vie for attention
Squirrels preparing as a warning
Soon it will be upon us, Winter

Winter and a forest turned white with frost
Mist drifts eerily between the trees
Thinking back through time it seems so close
Those fresh Spring days, halcyon Summer sun
The preparing for sleep time of Autumn

We start out in our Spring, our leaves unfurling
Maturity comes and we reach our Summer

Cease growing and our Autumn arrives
Winter brings an opportunity to re-thing, change
Seek the path of growth – experience eternal Spring!

Becoming

I am the life-giving sun
I am the fertile land
I am the fresh rain
I am the wild wind
I am the white snow
I am the rivers and sea
I am the living forest
I am the proud stag
I am the humble ant
I am the distant past
I am the unknown future
I am the gentle whale
I am the predatory lion
I am the wisdom of ages
I am the innocent baby
I am the black night sky
I am the sparkling stars
I am the welcome sunrise
I am the power to renew
I am divine
And so are you

Journey's End

Look within for answers
Always the only way
Seek YOUR truth and set YOURSELF free

Introspection long overdue
Inner mirrored
Seek YOUR truth and set YOURSELF free

Finally coming home
The you of you
Seek YOUR truth and set YOURSELF free...

Meet the Dream Stealers

They thought that they could rain on his parade
Thinking he listened to any of the points they made
How often they use words of anger, looking for a fight
Attempting to lead him from what he knows is right
Reminding him of supposed failures will never work
As the vitriol continues, with slander and a smirk

The dream stealers never achieve a thing
Nothing to be proud of makes their heart sing
Espying anyone moving forward in their life
Cuts through their senses like the sharpest knife
For dream stealers he has much compassion
Wishing they could share for life his passion

He knows exactly where he is going and how to
His vision of his future it is bright and it is true
Passionate thoughts fill his head, his dedication
Words showing all he visioned in his meditation
He learned so much, when things went askew
Changes to adapt his plan and continually renew

Who is Creating You?

Intellectual
Ineffectual
Tall
Small
Peasant
Pleasant
Older
Bolder
Reliable
Unreliable
Weird
Feared
Healing
Unfeeling
Visionary
Misery
Nationalist
Capitalist
Frightened
Enlightened

Labels imposed every day
No matter what others say
Transparently plain to see
We're creating our reality
Our thoughts beating like drums

Make sure they're always good ones
Our choice to choose our words
Their flight before us like birds
Live within peaceful emotion
Simple harmonic motion
Getting back what we give out
A truth beyond any doubt
The change you want is your choice
Attention to your quiet inner voice
Peace and Love purely given
The past laid to rest, forgiven
Gratitude for everything around
Then happiness has to abound
Anything feels wrong get rid of
Love to you, I wish you all Love

Summer Rain

To walk in the cleansing summer rain
Nirvana for humans and parched ground
Pine trees, roses, the damp earth
And a thousand other scents
All at once nature 's fragrances
Teasing senses with their beauty
Thoroughly soaking wet and caring not
Simple joys of being alive…

Far Horizons and One Love

Years spent looking for somewhere to call home
Fruitless search…wherever next to roam?
So many books absorbed in seeking inspiration
A million pages read for that certain revelation
Travelling far and wide always something missing
Wherever settling still niggling sense of misgiving
"Home is where the heart is" they often proclaim
Partially true yet there is more we need to regain
Journey to loving our essence of all we deeply are
Accepting the myriad of ourselves, however bizarre
All the great stuff along with all those faults as one
Reach this point, the journey home has now begun
It's not about a place, a person…well other than oneself
It's about an all-encompassing Love for yourself
Living at peace with all that makes you…well, you!
This is home…simply takes a different point of view
Being happy in our skin, everywhere feels like home
Constantly at home wherever we choose to roam…

The Element of Air

Southport pier and it was windy
Gale force 9 and then some
Hitting howlingly full face on
Second longest pier in England
So they say
Walking leaning at 45 degrees
Slowly progress is made
There is a destination
Seeing it through wind-made tears
Eventually, staggeringly
Making an entrance
And what a streaming eyed entrance
"Hi, may I have black coffee and toast"
The only customer in the café
Their only customer all morning
Being English they talked about the weather
What else to talk of today...
As the storm lashed their place of work
Rocking the whole structure as it creaks
Perhaps it was designed that way?
The café staff say they hope so
Sipping coffee
Frozen face thawing
The return journey pondered...

Cautiously heading towards the exit
Bidding farewell to fellow storm survivors
Wishing them well
Stepping outside
Still as crazy as ever out there
Full force hits squarely in the back
Propelled forward
Rapidly!
Go with the flow
Or get thrown face down onto the pier
Little choice in the end

All over in a blur of activity
That return walk
Positively at some point
Feet did genuinely leave the ground
At least for a few metres
The buzz of the experience remains
First nature and man had their battle
When no longer fighting her
The reward exceeded any roller-coaster ride

Sure, I looked like I'd survived a ship-wreck
Yet I felt euphoric…

Southport, Merseyside 2007

A true story of the author's battle with the elements inspired this tale

Stone-Proof

"Why I'm not feeling the energy, man?"
Hmmm this has to be a mystery
How does mysterious Avebury
Somehow mysteriously elude me…

Oh how I endeavoured to do the right thing
Even camped but a stones throw from the village
Walk the avenue of standing stones
Ensure I'm within the right energy

Continue around the circle of standing stones
Seemingly it doesn't matter
Clock or anti-clockwise
Still the identical outcome ensues

Hugging one particularly interesting standing stone
Closely like a long lost friend
Transcendent understanding now?
Nope, apparently I'm immune

I know the site has been messed about with
In the more recent past
Do the stones simply dislike my personal energy?
Who knows?

Paradoxically I adore the village of Avebury
Pub in the middle with well sunk right there inside
Enjoyed many a fine picnic sat amongst the stones
Meditated within the circle

The stones resolutely keep themselves to themselves
Consequently, for me it's always "No vibes, man"
Yet I always come away feeling better inside
Weird that, hey?

Stone circles always attract me

Final Rusting Place

Antony Gormley the genius responsible
 100 silent sentinels cast in iron looking out to sea
Crosby Beach their adopted home
Cast in the image of their creator so they say
Taking the waters twice a day…

Contemplation and introspection
Gaze westward more sentinels all at sea
Windmill blades turning
Providing power to the people
Work in harmony with nature and it rewards us

Nature rewards co-operation

The Busy Fool

Shoulder to the wheel
Nose to the grindstone
And all such other clichés
One dimensional ways
It's so easy to become the busy fool

Working fingers to the bone
Every waking hour
Does arduous work ensure success?
In some minds, yes
I guess

The busy fool
Hamster on wheel like
Chasing an illusion
Oh, how they graft in delusion
Oh, how in vain all the same

Weighed down
Crushed by life
Ploughing on regardless anyway
Automation's single pathway
Working like a trojan

Never seeing a reason
Choices

Always a choice…always a choice
Listen to that quiet inner voice
It's so easy to stop being a busy fool

Programming to undo
Passionately pursuing goals
Transformed within and without
"Treadmill existence farewell!" to shout
Living dreams…are you ready?

A choice

Fractured And Broken

Well I woke up this morning
Oh yeah, I woke up this morning
Been having this weird dream
At least I thought, can things be as they seem?
They wanna drill the Earth, fractured and broken
Are we supposed to believe a word these people spoken?

I got the fractured Earth blues
Oh yeah, the fractured Earth blues
Thinking what's the use?
Seems someone's gotta loose

Lookin' around on the net
They're doing it everywhere, what we get?
Earthquakes and tremors, flaming gas instead of water
Let's tell 'em what we think, it's really time we oughta
They're making their decisions profit before health
Changing geology forever and counting their wealth

I got the fractured Earth blues
Oh yeah, I got the fractured Earth Blues
Thinking what's the use?
Seems someone's gotta loose

How can we stop those insane actions?
Fracking apart the ground, chemical reactions

Make our voices heard loud and clear
Every time that new drilling rig starts to appear
Peaceful protest, reasoning don't work with these guys
Harder their job, less profit they make, let's open their eyes

I got the fractured Earth blues
Oh yeah, I got the fractured Earth Blues
Thinking what's the use?
Seems someone's gotta loose

Is my fracking blues song...the creative process never ceases to astound me. Why is it a blues song? It grew that way...

Labels

Which style of clothes we choose to wear
Are those designer labels on show there?
Or supermarket jeans with matching top
Did that bag come from an online shop?
Got to dress-up that look, make it "you"
Designer a must, branded training shoe

Myriad of gadgets await our pleasure
How exactly to enjoy our leisure?
Binned phone, new model pride of place
How is it better, this future we embrace?
Computers, pads, tablets, music storage devices
Plus the rest, of course, all at premium brand prices

Only one way to be totally able
Free yourself from any kind of label

We used to buy a car for what it did
A choice that brand awareness then undid
If it doesn't wear the proper badge it's tragic
Of course, it's nice to have nice things, magic
Buying into designer experience is only a sham
For sure an Emperor's New Clothes kind of scam

What is your job, who is your circle?
How to exist in the world most commercial?

How is your accent, are you eloquent enough?
Are you geeky or perhaps considered hot stuff?
Wearing shades in winter only for the look
Posting to impress to excess on facebook

Only one way to be totally able
Free yourself from any kind of label

Look within for the answers to our life
Chasing labels the cause of so much strife
Look within for the answer always been inside
Let intuition now be our eternal guide
Happiness our birthright, to be free of
Chasing labels and just feeling the love

Inspired (if that is the right word!) by two young women I overheard talking about designer labels in a clothes boutique, how some jeans which the very paragon of fashion last Spring, are today really a little tragic to seen in…

Quantum Stairway

Stood on the middle step of the stairs
Ascend or descend?

Eternal decision to make...

All Roads Leading to the Eternal Now

PART ONE – So Many Changes

Born into this World of mystery
Exploring into greater understanding
Schooling according to someone else's plan
Nature teaching infinitely more
Night sky fascinates
Stars and moon familiar friends
Healing others in innocence

Rediscovering who I am
Telling others of my dreams
Falling mainly upon closed ears
Yet keeping the dreams all the same
Forth into adulthood
Career paths to take
The dreams remain

Maturity of responsibility
Others depend upon my labours
Co-workers looking upon me as vital
Still I seek more
I love words and healing
My dreams entice me

Always the dreams
Dreams there to be followed
The past to be forgiven
In deepest gratitude for the journey
Oh to heal with words
Inspire, just as words inspire
More changes yet I am constant
Life changes, I grow

PART TWO - The Boots

Walking boots are donned early morn
Into nature witness the rising dawn
Spring Solstice what could inspire more?
Forgotten stone circle upon empty moor
Coolness felt upon my essentially bare feet
Eyes closed, sense sunrise, harmony complete
Warming rays invigorating body and soul
Oneness with all elements at once whole

PART THREE – Realisation

Sometimes introspection
Sometimes isolation
Ultimate revelation
Ultimate elation
Transcendent inspiration
Transcendent realisation

PART FOUR – Heart and Soul

A higher purpose for existing
Forever seeking, persisting
Look within and look without end
Make yourself your own best friend
Sincerely wish to know, it's up to you
Know the truth and then what to do
My truth took a while to sink in
Inner voice screaming, making a din
Time for my heart to overrule my head
My mission in life was to widely spread
Word of love inner understanding
Minds perhaps a little expanding
I hope with all my heart and soul
That you will also find your role…

This is my "prog-rock" poem and was inspired by those great 1970's lyrical wizards with their concept triple-albums…I poetically salute you all and hope my contribution to the genre is accessible to all who read…

It's the Short-Term Memory

The vertigo I ignore
Mal de mer existence
The room sways a little
Flip flopping the horizon
I get on with living

Headaches…also ignored
No, the bigger challenge
Memory…short term memory
Everything written down
On not one…
But two notepads!
Lest it be forgotten
Words acting as triggers
Connecting neural pathways

And they ask why I never plan
Always seem to wing it
I work within parameters
I work with what I have
I work spontaneously
I work the only way which works
I work on living a full life
I am fearless
I jump in with both feet
Then see where I landed

Saying Yes to opportunities
When they present themselves
Which they always do
Always

Live big...live large
Live
Yes...life
How often taken for granted
Precious life
So many things to do
New horizons
Opportunities to grow

And a legacy
I feel that stronger now
Never sought fame
Although it found me
Well, perhaps a little
It's all about legacy
I did this
I spoke those words
I wrote those words
This is me...I did that

As I focus on the choices
Threefold adventures
Poetry, performance...living!
Yet perhaps not so different

Oh yes...it's all about
Living...

Asking Questions

It took a while
Well okay, a goodly few decades
Looking outwards observing life
Pondering inwardly
When the student is ready

I know the answer
Oh finally, the truth is revealed
The great unanswered mystery
A "How to" manual to life
Well, it's about...questions

Every time we think
We ask ourselves questions
Even opting out of decisions
First requires we ask of us
A question

What to do then?
If to transcend the treadmill existence
The answer is crystal clear
Still ask ourselves questions
But, make them amazing ones!

To stretch comfort zones
Be in The Zone

Raising our standards
Expectations of outcomes
Firstly, ask ourselves amazing questions

Amazing questions
More amazing answers
Unparalleled amazing life
Dare to dare ourselves the only way
The quality of questions to us...is all

Men of Vision

Where have all the great engineers gone?
Brunel, Thomas Telford and George Stephenson
Men of vision creating a legacy to last
Are the best inventions all now in the past?

Making railways, ships of iron, train of steam
These men one and all followed their dream
By mathematics and physics, they planned
No computer graphics to help them understand

With cutting edge technology and design
Geniuses of Victorian Age, way ahead of their time
Bridges and tunnels still in use even to this day
Can we really say the same of what is built today?

I love the ingenuity of the industrial revolution; this poem celebrates these amazing pioneers and laments the lack of romance in their 21st century colleagues endeavours

They Only Want To Farm

It started in the eighteenth century in the Highlands of Scotland
Lairds decreed "uneconomical tenant farmers throw them from
their land!"
And so the clearances began, buildings burning, shameful enough
to make you weep
It took some seventy years to clear them all and making way for
only sheep

1970's a new decade, economic boom, prosperity, everyone has a
car
Let's build new roads, lots of motorways, to take us wide and far
Government policy, if a farm should be in our way, go build
anyway
Cars are more important, give farmers some money, they'll go
away

Dawning of a new century, farmers' wondering what the future
could bring
At the mercy of supermarkets pricing wars; they never could have
predicted the next thing
Drilling rigs appearing all around the land, fracking, poisoning
the crops that feed
Farmers once again the victims of powerful people's greed

This poem came about when I read of a farmer having to allow a fracking mega-corporation onto his land, regardless of if he wished them to be there…which in this case he certainly didn't!

Growers of the crops around the world, I poetically salute you!

Written On A Beach

Well North East girls are hip
Barely any clothes they ever wear
And the Essex girls well the way they talk
With their orange skin and bleached blonde hair

The Devon farmer's daughters really keep you up all night
And Macclesfield girls with the way they kiss
They give their boyfriends such a fright

I wish they all could be East European
I wish they all could be East European
I wish they all could be East European girls

With more than a nod to a certain surf influenced band who started their journey in the early 1960's

Three Galleries In A Day

Friday, five o-clock train, journey underway
An idea, tomorrow do three galleries in a day!
A schedule like that should be all planned out, I agree
Not the way I do things, rather "let's just wait and see"

Leaving my hostel at eight thirty to Southbank I venture
Thus, begins the opening gallery of my one day adventure
Dali Universe, thrilling…I love his work and abstract mind
Melting clocks, lip shaped sofas, a hundred sketches combined
Picasso exhibition in the basement, adding to the pleasure
Two hours spent there. It's time for my next endeavour

Walking east along Southbank, The Tate Modern stands proud
Umpteen times I've been here, my enthusiasm still unbowed
I adore surrealists, I love dada, a little of modern arts Masterpieces
made from litter or old bicycle parts
Three metre canvass painted purest black, made me almost faint
What was the artist thinking "wish I had some different paint?" A
Citroen van rusting in peace and pieces is it a joke?
Perhaps like some of the other art it's only there to provoke?

A thousand paintings, sculptures and visual arts I've seen
Next gallery please, to the National Portrait Gallery I convene Past
Trafalgar Square, culture lays there awaiting
Never experienced before, excitedly anticipating
Okay I have to confess portraiture not really quite my thing

Got to visit nonetheless, with traditional art I'll have a fling
The first few paintings I observe...admire the brushwork?
Even a surrealist philistine like me can see it took a lot of work A
hundred portraits later, each one beginning to look alike
Bored stiff, tired, thinking it's about time I took a hike
Spying a comfy chair, coffee machine, sitting peacefully
Taking a few moments, fall deeply asleep unbelievably...

For two hours I lay snoring, until finally I awoke
When in my ear the guard of the gallery gently spoke
"Sir we close in fifteen minutes, please leave!"
Looking at the time defied anything I could believe
Less than twenty minutes left my train was going
Running along Tottenham Court Road dignity forgoing
Only just...I got there...with two minutes to spare
Of these ridiculous situations it seems I have the flair

Still as I sat there travelling back, reflecting, pondering
I loved my time in London, wandering and wondering

*A London visit back in 2006, although the poem was written later from
my notes*

Again, The Moon Full

It was a clear night as the Moon looked down with apathy upon
the dwellers on the city
Going about their important tasks with intense intent, feeling a
sense of inner pity
Meaningful and yet oh so meaningless, trying to make sense of it
all
Fit everything into the quantum soup, existence in this urban
sprawl
Such strange ingredients to work with. Moon, what say you?
Do those lost souls floating on a cloud, make you feel blue?
Our bodies borrowed from the Universe, a billion years old
Yet renewing every moment. What will history say when our
story is told?

*Incredibly I have written four poems on the theme of the full moon
looking down on humanity, this is the second in the series of the poem!*

Camping In The English Summer

Camping a must…makes the experience unforgettable
On internet campsite chosen a decision later regrettable
Basic is the kindest way I could describe the alleged facilities Mud
and lots of it, derelict shower block, medieval utilities Pitched our
tent, make the best of it, one good meal enjoyed Darkness falls,
warm sleeping bag, our peace soon destroyed Wildest storm
torrentially blows, flapping canvass, precipitation
"Will we be okay, tell me we'll be fine" I'm asked for confirmation
"Yeah, of course we will, we're dry and safe, all is sweet"
Diplomatically not mentioning my soaking wet feet…

Funnily enough we did go camping again after this experience! (2015)

Just the Model

"Just walk naturally down the catwalk"
How exactly? For me not exactly a cakewalk
Doing a favour for a friend taking on new meaning
How did I get involved in this? What was I dreaming?
Time to confess, what I had agreed to that fateful day
A Bridal Fayre! Yes, I know, you don't have to say!
I had to pretend to be a groom and then walk a bit
Fine until I saw who I was paired with, then "oh…my!"
My bride for the whole event, my partner, was fair Carrie
So fond of one another we barely talked, never mind marry
The director said "walk to the end and then you two kiss"
"What?!" This is one our friends would not want to miss
Being professional, not wishing to spoil the event
Walk we did and the kiss we couldn't circumvent
We closed our eyes, did the deed, our friends laughing horribly
Carrie and I managing to not look too repulsed, erm…probably
How many more wedding dresses do they want Carrie to parade?
Oh great! Only another four more times to go…my day is made
Said to the director "can I not change partners, have a different
"wife"?"
She looked at me in horror "our brides and grooms are together
for life"
I still have the flashbacks sometimes, waking expecting to see
Carrie
Maybe the trauma of that event is why I never chose to marry?

What happens when you say yes, and then find yourself wondering why you did...I need to add that I do rhyme the name Carrie with marry twice! Fortunately, she does have a name that fits into a poem rather well and yes, we really did once have such an incredibly well developed mutual distaste for one another's company...although we were professional on the day

A Journey Too Far

It seemed like a good idea, the invitation inviting
Join the club for cycling, really rather exciting
The local newspaper said, 3rd Tuesday of the Month, come along
Share your stories, have a chat, join our happy throng

Full of fine intentions, my journey now well underway
The club my destination to arrive soon without delay
Then snowing, then sleeting, then a little more snow
Turning back never occurred, onwards we will go!

Thinking as I got there, do they not have another member?
It's so quiet, could it be because this is the 24th of December?
Knocking on the door to be greeted by deafening silence
A community centre very closed, in spite of my defiance

To ride back appears my only option now
My hands and feet so chilled, I wonder how?
No feeling in my fingers, like they might break
The journey home I now begin to undertake

A little more sleet, just to help my on my way
The words I thought to myself, I wouldn't care to say
Praying I would have no reason to pull up sharp or stop
If I had to use my frozen fingers, sure I'd faint and drop

Peddling along against the wind, my racing bike crawled home
With every extreme of icy weather feeling more alone
'Till finally our driveway, a more welcome sight I never saw
Three long and very painful hours it took for me to finally thaw!

If some new adventure or interest you espy
The moral of this story is clear for all to learn by
Even if seems perfection and everything in which you believe
By all means go find out more, but never on Christmas Eve

This story happened many years ago and my teenage self takes centre-stage for this poem, the memory of the day remains strongly imprinted upon my mind

Some People

Some people take themselves terribly seriously
These people are to be avoided at all costs
Apparently, they give off toxic fumes…

Some people only like the sound of their own voice
These people are to be avoided at all costs
Apparently, their ears are malfunctioning…

Some people have their headphones so loud all can hear
These people are to be avoided at all costs
Apparently, they always have terrible taste in music…

Some people are concerned with only how they look
These people are to be avoided at all costs
Apparently, their heads are quite hollow…

An extremely gentle rant

Mistaken Identity

Part One

How to react and how should I greet?
When "hello Paul" is called from across the street
Thinking they mistook me for some friend they know
Pretending I hadn't heard and on my way I go
Until the day I ventured to Morecambe town
"Hello Paul" I heard again, two guys looking at me with a frown
"Why do you not answer?" one asked loudly, quite aggressively
"Hi guys! Sorry, I was miles away" while I smiled inoffensively
Being mistaken for Paul continued for more than half a year
Exactly who Paul is or was never did become quite clear

Part Two

Whilst in a well-known store the name of which I shan't mention
Well, ok it was Wilkinson's, a bargain being my intention
"Hello Daddy" a small child called out, looking me in the eyes
Glancing behind to make sure she meant me, hiding my surprise
Her orange hued mother turning a bright shade of red
Smiling weakly at me, her expression full of dread
What to answer? I'm pretty sure I'd never met mum before
A quick "Sorry, not me" and escape to the first floor?
Her mum saved me from further awkwardness arisen
"You know that can't be daddy, he's locked up in prison!"

Two stories, which although separated by a few years, nevertheless both saw me being taken for someone else

Boots 3

On the cold winters morning thermal boots are pulled on
The radio announced…ground frost and the promise of snow later
in the day
And yet she is happy…
Happy because she is doing what she loves
The market is freezing in December
Icy winds blow and there is no sunlight to warm frozen hands
It's the people you see
Fellow workers on the market, pleased to see her
Customers stopping by to give her a cup of tea
Camaraderie and friendship being formed over the selling of
clothes
For years she was part of the rich tapestry that makes Preston
market special
Until illness took her away
Even her thermal boots could not help her
If you walk through Preston market one cold December day
Say hello…although you won't see her as you pass on your way
It's keeping a tradition alive you see…everyone said hello to her

My mum's mother, we called her nan, worked on Preston outdoor market
all year round

Totally Fitness

All hail to those who come to worship at the temple
The temple of the body beautiful, with a strain and tremble
Music pumping, yet not really noticed
As bodies are pumping, to be noticed
Machines activated by human power
Working up a sweat "just another hour"
Seeking to become just a little more physically decked
Body mass index and calorie counting minutely checked
Gaining bulging muscles or loosing bulges they want to shed
Weighing scales their best friend or looked at with utter dread
I too used to worship at the temple a long time ago
I've looked at life from both sides now and for me I know
Thank, but looking at these guys I don't see any smiles
Exercise is wonderful, viewing beautiful scenery, I walk for miles

I found myself in a branch of an extremely well-known fitness chain for a children's party of all things, thankfully I had my trusty notebook and pen with me (2013)

Fast-Food Now!

Of course, he looked like a clown.
And yet he was also incredibly clever
The clown being an illusion
To fool people into thinking he was harmless
This amused him
That most of the population only saw the façade
And no further
It was all part of his insidious plan
Soon everyone would know him
From Brighton Rock to Borneo...Japan to Milan

He sat there in his ridiculous outfit
With it's big shoes and the red nose
And thought over the last few years
How his genius knew no bounds
His plan working perfectly
He chuckled, for once sounding like a real clown
Thinking about how gullible the public were
How easily they fell for all the hype
The hype, with no real substance behind it
Yes, *onald *c*onald had every reason to be happy

A poem I simply had to write!

Boots 5

Climbing boots are pulled on early morn
He'd been up since the first sign of dawn
Three fellow free-climbing nutcases on a mission
To climb the waterfall at Mallam their ambition
Travelling light, no need to use any rope
A speedy ascent, safely, their hope

One man volunteers "I'm going to make a start"
Up the rockface he climbed, completing the first part
Then came the trickier bit, climbing up the very waterfall
His friends stood and watched, four metres high…the fall
His hand slipping on wet stone, scrabbling for a moment…feels
like forever
No rope to break his descent, backwards he fell, despite his best
endeavour
Hitting the ground with a thud, his friends rushing to assist
"Are you ok", "Talk to us". With a grin their help he dismissed
He went to sit in their van, a cup of coffee and then try again
After thirty minutes he'd finished his rest, he tried to move…pain
Argh he thought and ahh as well, he seems he couldn't stand or
walk
Calling rather loudly to his friends "Guys, I think we need to
talk!"
They took him to get checked out, it seems he'd damaged his
spine

The shock of falling, adrenalin having made everything seem just fine

Physiotherapy following, the art of walking now regained
"Now I'm recovering, I shall climb again!" he proclaimed
Geology interested him, so to a quarry he did venture
Keep it safe he thought, for my first new adventure
Alone he went this time, he was just going to have a wander
Long way by the footpath he found his way round yonder

To the very top of the cliff, on scree he slipped and…towards the edge he went
Until his rock hammer he slammed in the ground, to stop his quick descent
All his weight taken on one arm for a full hour, slowly he found solid ground
How to get back with a dislocated shoulder and nobody else around?
The journey was "interesting" to say the least, his shoulder was fixed
Climbing boots are pulled on early morn, with feelings that are mixed
He still loves the mountains, the feeling of freedom, just the rock and him
Maybe he will climb again one day, if he can do it without breaking a limb!

Boots, the series of poems featuring my ancestors, is brought up to date with a little of my own story

Apparently, I'm Not Scottish

I get invited sometimes for the occasional interview
This time in Aberdeen, without much thought I flew
"We'll pick you up" they said "to take you to the studio"
Quickly my lift arrived, and he asked if I'm ready to go?
Upon my reply, hearing my accent, he stopped in his tracks
"You're not a Scottish Fraser, you're a wee Sassenach!"
"Erm…actually my roots are Celtic French not Scots see"
"Frasier became Fraser some time ago, you understand mais oui?"
He failed to laugh. He growled "we thought you were one of us"
"Don't think we need you in our studio, nothing for us to discuss"
Standing there open mouthed, trying to take this in my stride
Am I allowed to hit him? No, the dignified exit I decide
Scotland…I love the place…I've even worn the Fraser plaid
From the brief encounter in Aberdeen at least I still got paid

*A more or less true story, I wouldn't be a poet if I didn't occasionally use
a little poetic license…the exact facts have been altered to protect the
slightly ignorant gentleman concerned, who was forgiven long ago!*

Inside The Boots

I sit here thinking about my poetry collectively known as Boots
What they mean to me and what exactly are our roots?
Do these ancestors I write about feel like a part of me?
Did these people somehow collectively define who I would be?

In this life do we live by our own free will choice?
Is it wise to be quiet and listen to the inner voice?
The advice of others even with the best of intentions
However well meaning, I've found often leads to tensions

The question, is our destiny truly our own to decide?
Does to follow other than destiny, cause planets to collide?
Could it be our life is planned out before we are even born?
Do we always have to smell the rose and also grip the thorn?

Does making decisions and forging ahead enthusiastically
Achieve any more than those who wait there passively?
Are we the total sum of the DNA that is our inheritance?
Perhaps who we are is based purely on our own experience?

To think that everything before us is completely pre-ordained
What motivation to get out of bed? Life would be so pained
For what it's worth I believe our future is very ours to make
What I choose to call learning, others may see as mistakes

Poetically pondering my own poetry…erm and writing a poem about said pondering

All Part Of The Plan Blues

Looking around and wondering how it all happened
Once familiar buildings with character now flattened
Identikit high streets, which town is it I'm in again?
It's so easy to get confused, how to stay sane?
Got to thinking, progress happens so they say
Connected to the electronic superhighway
No need to walk and visit the private retailers
Buy it all from faceless internet purveyors

Frank's fish and chip shop closed ten years back
International fast food outlets moved in to fill the lack
Serving their mass produced synthetic pseudo-food
Everything designed to put us in a buying mood
Superstores killing towns and cities their main mission
Green belt being lost to retail parks, whatever opposition
Buy everything you need… your shopping, insurance, don't be
shy
Get your holidays, car, glasses, photos…they'll even bury you if
you die

Where will it all end, change has already happened, what more?
There's no going back, that's for sure, we already closed that door
But these giant stores create jobs, this is what the politicians say
Yet surely a high street full of independent shops, people could
earn their pay?
Tiny little malls seem to be the way of the small shop owner

Some kind of mini retail theme park, down want to sound like a downer
But they used to be on the High Street and weren't called quaint and cute
Although that they have been able to adapt is at least astute

They say, the past is nice to visit but you wouldn't want to live there
Just seems to me some things were once better if we dare compare
Do we have to follow the American Dream with quite such passion?
Can being ourselves, with our own identity not be the fashion?
Okay I guess it's come the time to end this little ditty
Social commentary about every town and city
If it sounded like a rant, well I suppose it can be said it is
Sharing a few thoughts with you all as I care to reminisce

Are some things truly better now?

Every Day A Celebration

Remember, Remember…the what of November?
Was sure there was something…try to remember
Dates in a diary reminders of significance
Sure there was something…just think perchance
Perchance to think…or was it sleep?
Or is perchancing to think altogether too deep?
Ahhh good old computer the answers I seek
To google or not? I'll just have a peek
November is Vegan Month…hurray!
I'm writing this on Author's Day…way hay!
Does it get any better than this I hear you all say
It does! Wow! 6th November is Saxophone Day!
Yet I still think I'm missing something what can it be?
Google some more and I'm sure I'll see…
Could it be the fact that on the 7th November men are supposed
to cook?
Men Cook Dinner Day…hmmm…that's one I shall accidently
overlook
11th November forever special…not many days in celebration of
origami!

Except even better 12th is Pizza Day, with the works except
anchovy
Just in time for 15th…Clean Your Refrigerator Day it's official
I suppose after all that pizza it's probably beneficial
Who decides these days has clearly thought it through

To name all these days was definitely overdue
20th November is Name your PC Day and those are the facts
I named mine Meryl...after that great woman who acts
Shopping Reminder Day is 26th November...do we need
reminding to spend?
Less than one Month to go to the fateful day...will it ever end?
Dates to remember and some to forget
Fond memories are made, some to regret
How wonderful the 29th a day to remember to floss
Why nobody thought of that before I'm at a loss
I see from google that December is incredible
Why do people always eat sprouts, they're inedible?
But no, it's not about that, presents or religion
You'll have to think laterally just a wee bit of a smidgeon
December I cannot keep to myself, I have to tell you why
December is International Month to Wear a Tie!

*I wrote this for a Guy Fawkes Night poetry event back in 2013, I include
it here because it still makes me smile...*

2008 Blackpool – Riverdance Comes To Town

She was in trouble, navigating the extreme weather
She was going to end up beached, no choice whatsoever
Crashing, breaking in the waves, the end was inevitable
Brave men rescuing everyone, scenes unforgettable
Gale force winds howling like a banshee
Tilting a crazy angle, will she be lost to sea?
Riverdance the ship, there she lay on the beach
Would they manage to float her again, with the hull breach?
As she sat there rusting in peace
They cut her up, piece by piece
That year visitors to Blackpool found a new attraction to go see
Every other venue in the town takes cash, the ship was free!
An attraction in the town that cost no money to view
In the very ethics of the place it rang untrue
To the salvage crew they told their plan
Get this ship away from here just as fast as you can
Bit by bit, over a few short months she was gone
Now paying fun the tourists can focus upon
If my rhyme does sound a trifle satirical
It's not really, I'm completely non-political
Merely an observer of life and people's motivations
That Riverdance went so quickly I offer congratulations
The story of the ship which found itself beached a little up the coast from central Blackpool (2013)

Egotistical Me

Ego often being confused with self-belief...
Self-knowing...
Self-love
There being a world of difference
Taking action for recognition...
And because one has to
In order to change...evolve
Leave behind that which no longer serves
I had my peacock years
Oh vanity thy name was Dean...

Your friendly poet back in his corporate days...eek! My earlier self,
looked at from the benefit of distanc

This Is Reality, Babe

Is there no escape from the horror?
No exit sign for this intrepid explorer?
Been here so long, can't remember life before
Will it go away if I close my eyes and just ignore?
No, it's still there in all too concrete reality
Glass and steel, executed excessive brutality
Soulless, stark bleakness everywhere
Zombie like people, do they actually care?
Everything, the sights, the sounds totally banal
As I spend the afternoon "shopping" in the mall

Help!

Glasson Dock Or Twilight Zone?

"The short cut can save us some time" I said
If only I could have foreseen what lay ahead!
Past the farm, oh yes, we were saving time and how
The pathway narrowed, turning the corner, the killer cow!
Her and her friends marching towards us without a halt
We turned and sprinted faster than Usain Bolt
Half a mile we ran back past the farm of their destination
The farmer and his son laughing loudly at our desperation

Leaping over a gate, back on the marsh, getting our breath back
For finding these strange situations it seems we do have a knack
Walking a little further, eventually it came in sight
Pleasure yachts glistening appealingly in the light
Down the road we sallied forth with a smile
Which sadly lasted for rather less than a mile
Young gentleman outside a pub shouting across to us
No idea what they said, we didn't stay around to discuss

A café we espied, I suggested "let's take a few moments to rest"
To be greeted by "We're closed!" I said "Surely you must jest?"
She pointed us across the bridge, to a lovely mobile café
Well ok, it was an old caravan, hey it might be great, who can say?
The teenagers queuing with us must be locals was our conclusion
Unless them wearing only socks and no shoes was just an illusion

We got served eventually and ordered our coffee, taken black
Black being essential, of any other choice there was a lack

Deciding departure from this place was long overdue now
Off we set of a more direct way back to the car and how!
Walking for about an hour and a plane circling overhead
Suddenly five people falling in the sky, we stop and stared in dread
Will we have to administer first aid? Well, this is certainly our belief
Parachutes open and safely they descend, much to our relief
We will go back again some day, just not maybe on our own!
And see if Glasson Dock really is…The Twilight Zone

A visit to this small Lancashire coastal town (or is it a village?) became weirder with every passing hour (2013)

Re-Invention Is Alive Here...Bristol

Archibald Leach he once answered to
Leaving these shores
United States of America
Life anew
Pathway to fame and fortune
Adored
Celluloid sophistication personified
Universally Cary Grant

David Prowse
Physical perfection
Bodybuilder...British champion
Face of road safety
In half forgotten bygone days
Achieving fame and anonymity
Seen but not heard
Darth Vader

A music degree
Piano and flute
Perfect qualifications?
Perhaps they are after all?
Engineering expertise
Intellect sits alongside irony

Walking talking contradiction
That is James May

Man of mystery
Hails from Bristol
So they say
Urbanity his canvass
Art loud and proud
For the people
Making his mark, his statement
Yet who is Banksy?

Touching base in the end
Another famous son
Pioneer
Game changing visionary
Jodrell Bank the place
Standing proud and still relevant
Perhaps more than ever
Sir Bernard Lovell…I wish I had met you

This was originally going to be a far longer poem telling of those famous people hailing from Bristol…and then I reached a point where I believed the story I wanted tell was done and so we end with Sir Bernard

The Name Is Moore

A sardonic smile and a raised eyebrow
Communicating volumes somehow
Body language scaled down to one eye
Contempt, love, hello or goodbye

Homage to a hero of mine

Talking to Myself

As I observe, I feel I need to ask myself "Why is it that people talk without thinking first?"

I see it everywhere I venture, people creating their very own version of hell and I wonder "Why would they do that? Make their life so limited and one dimensional?"

Further pondering on the matter drew me to further observe "They ask for exactly what they don't want, all the time, why would they think that is good?"

I have to admit I believe I do know the answer to that question. The answer is quite clear. Ignorance of the truth and ignorance is very rarely bliss.

It is part of every doctrine, every religion, every philosophy, every metaphysical knowledge, quantum physics, occultism...ok, you get the idea, all the wise ones say the same...You ARE what you think...Words resonate through time and space forever.

Pondering (2013)

Croatia

Jagoda, Krumpir
Dobro, Molim
Zastava, Da
Kikiriki, Hrvatska
Volim Te, Ciao
Vlak, Oko
Grudi, Moda

Strawberry, Potato
Good, Please
Flag, Yes
Peanut, Croatia
I love you, Hello
Train, Eye
Breast, Fashion

This one always sounds impressive when I perform it…I provide the
translation so it all makes sense (or not!) I enjoy having this one in my
live set

What?

Tomorrow will be yesterday in two days...yesterday was tomorrow two days ago...the only possible reality is NOW...everything else is just past/future tense...

Makes perfect sense to me! Yes, really!!!

Are You Ready?

Spend your life dreaming about trivia and that's what you end up
with
Make your dreams big ones...big, bold and in glorious
technicolour
Paint them across your imagination and go wild.
And if the dream is possible, however remotely, there is a good
chance the way will be made available to achieve your dream.
It will happen...the choice is then yours...how much do you want
it? and how brave do you feel?
life will change.
Are you ready?

*Philosophical poetry...and big dreams are the only kind worth going for
really*

Poem in 45 Seconds...

Come have our credit card
It's always easy, never hard
Buy all you want, here's two grand limit
No need to save, have it now, be with it
Until the day reality hits home
It's just another form of loan
Monthly statement shows the sums
And then the payback comes

Guess how long this one took to write? About the same amount of time it takes to apply for a credit card online

Sam Spode (Gumshoe)

It had to rain. In this dirty town, on these mean streets, it always had to rain. Maybe the mayor didn't pay a big enough bribe to the big guy, so it rained. The kind of rain that filled the gutters and made stepping off the sidewalk like paddling in the Hudson.

I was parked in my heap across the way from a bookstore. Well, what's a gumshoe supposed to do? I was being paid real well by a dame with dyed red hair and legs all the way to ground and she didn't mind who saw them. "I want you to watch my husband, he runs Dirks' the bookstore on the corner of 53rd and 8th". She produced a roll of bills and threw them on my blotter. I said "Sure lady, what's the sap supposed to have done?". She looked at me like I'd crawled from under a dirty stone "That's what I'm paying you to find out!"

I sat and watched. You'll do a lot of that in my line of work, comes with the turf, like stomach ulcers and cheap bourbon. The rain leaking in through my heaps door onto my shoulder and feet didn't make me in any better kinda mood.

Just when I was deciding this bookworm dude was gonna be a waste of my $10 an hour time, the door of the shop opened and out walked my "mark", along with the kinda blonde you see on movie posters and from the way they were getting along I'm thinking she wasn't his long-lost maiden aunt.

Time for the sap to pose for some real nice family photos. Now I ain't no Man Ray, but I know which way to point a camera to get evidence. I sighed to myself. Another divorce case. I took my photos and then thought about following the happy "couple", then I thought again. If this guy's dumb enough to carry on in his own shop, he's gonna carry on being predictably dumb and take her to the nearest nickel and dime motel.

I saved myself the trouble of tailing them, found a phone and called Mad Manny at Fingers O'Keefe's Motel on 65th. Sure enough my sap had booked a room and was just checking in. I drove over there like I had all the time in the World, real leisurely like. Parked my heap and sauntered in. Manny grunted at me through cheap cigar smoke and when I produced folding stuff he gave me his pass key.

I went up to the 3rd floor and made my gentle way along to room 39. Pressed my ear against the door and could hear gasps of pleasure coming from inside. I inserted the pass key in the door as quietly as I could, I'm sure they didn't hear it four blocks away.

Opened the door. There were books everywhere and my sap was just explaining to the dame that this was a signed first edition of the Time Machine by HG Wells and if she wanted to buy it all for herself it was gonna cost her two hundred green ones.

Just my luck, no quick easy divorce case. Some smart-ass dude selling rare books, without putting them through his books.

I walked out of the Motel with plenty of folding reasons to keep quiet. I'd tell the saps wife he ain't having no affair and he'd not have to give her his house in alimony.

Justice. It's what I do in this mean town.

Not quite sure why I wrote this, although I suspect it's because I wanted to read the story! I see a future movie in this one and merchandising, lots of merchandising. Well okay, maybe not, still nice to get it out into print at long last

Printed in Poland
by Amazon Fulfillment
Poland Sp. z o.o., Wrocław